# Contents

**4 Landscapes of Corsica**

*Poggio-di-Venaco from the D40 (Walk 9)*

#  Preface

Corsica is often referred to as the 'Isle of Beauty', or the 'Scented Isle'; both are very fitting, but I'd like to propose another name: the 'Friendly Isle'. The constant friendliness of the Corsicans towards me outshone all else. Unlike most tourist resorts, it was the rule rather than the exception. Renting an apartment was more like staying with friends than a business affair, and asking for directions ended up in friendly chats, before being lead to my path. And perhaps most extraordinary of all: friendly and helpful tourist offices (*syndicats d'initiative*)! A rarity in the world of tourism. Corsica, I discovered, is unique!

No other Mediterranean island can boast such a wealth of natural beauty. Beaches to suit every taste: from long stretches of glaring white sand to pink rocky coves. *Real* mountains — climbers' terrain — that reach almost 3000m/9000ft. In these mountains you stumble upon a magnificent mixture of pine forests, beech woods, chestnut groves, and coppices of evergreen oaks. Streams bound down the mountainsides; rivers cascade through awe-inspiring gorges, leaving behind blue-green pools as clear as crystal. The pink granite hills and cliffs, normally conjured up only for an artist's canvas, are real indeed on Corsica. In spring the countryside is enlivened with a tapestry of wild flowers and maquis in bloom. The hills are ablaze with colour; the air is intoxicatingly scented by the maquis.

For history buffs, the island is littered with evidence of its turbulent past, dating from about 6000BC. Rudimentary megalithic monuments still lie where they were placed thousands of years ago — in fields and out in the maquis-clad hills. The severe and simple Romanesque churches draw you to a halt with the precision of their masonry. Enchanting, story-book villages, many dating from the Middle Ages, adorn the landscape. They perch atop rocky spurs or high on mountainsides, enjoying 'belvedere' views.

The sheer unspoilt beauty of Corsica is enough to turn anyone into an explorer, be it on foot or by car. Driving around, you get itchy feet just looking at the never-ending beauty spots. You may not be a walker, but you'll soon find yourself wandering off into the countryside. The short walks and picnic suggestions will lure you from your vehicle into the magnetic landscape. Nowhere will you get more pleasure out of walking, whether you choose a short stroll or you tackle the GR20. Driving is equally enjoyable. Corsica is still far from flooded with tourists, as your tours in the countryside will prove. Crossing vast uninhabited tracts of land, you often pass more livestock than vehicles.

Corsica cannot guarantee you the eternal sunshine of, say, the Canaries — or even the prolonged summer of most of the Mediterranean islands. So if it's swimming and sunning you're after, visit Corsica in high season. But if walking is your priority, go in spring for the flowers or in autumn when the trees are turning colour and the shepherds are returning to the valleys with their flocks.

I hope that, armed with *Landscapes of Corsica*, you will discover the real island, and its friendly face.

— NOEL ROCHFORD

## Acknowledgements

For help with the preparation of the First and Second editions of this book, warm thanks to the French Tourist Office, L'Agence Régionale du Tourisme, Le Parc Naturel Régional de la Corse, l'Office National des Forêts, and various *syndicats d'initiative* throughout Corsica. Unfortunately I have not been able to return to Corsica for several years. Many thanks to my publishers at Sunflower, John and Pat Underwood, for preparing the greatly-revised third edition and all subsequent editions.

## Recommended books and maps
### Guides
Apart from the ubiquitous Rough Guides and Lonely Planet, we recommend: the *Eyewitness Guide to Corsica* (Dorling Kindersley), *Corsica* (Cadogan Guides), *Guide Vert: Corse* (Michelin, in French)
*Le Guide Corse de la Corse* (tourist booklet available on the island, from local *syndicats d'initiative* (in French only)
Parc Naturel Régional de la Corse guides to the island's flora, etc (available on Corsica, in French)
Office National des Forêts guides to forestry walks (available on Corsica, in French)

### Background reading
Dorothy Carrington: *Granite Island: a portrait of Corsica* (Penguin)

### Maps
*For touring:* Michelin map No 345 (*Corse-du-Sud, Haute-Corse*); scale 1:150,000
*For walking:* IGN 'Top 25' maps (scale 1:25,000; 19 sheets covering the whole of Corsica); available from your local map stockist and in bookshops, kiosks and petrol stations all over the island

# ❀ Getting about

Corsica is a large island indeed, and the public transport network is limited, especially outside high season. The problem is best solved by hiring a vehicle for either part or all of your vacation. Some package holidays have very good **fly/drive** arrangements, so do investigate these.

The SNCF runs a good **train** service connecting Ajaccio, Corte, l'Ile-Rousse, Calvi, and Bastia. This is an excellent way to see the interior of the island and reach the mountain walks. The railway tracks and rolling stock are being thoroughly modernised as we go to press; all work will be finished by 2010.

Local **buses** are always fun, but are few and far between. Tourists will find them mostly unsuitable, since scheduling serves the needs of the local community (eg, mail or school buses). In the high season (July to September), however, there are some special 'tourist route' buses which are more helpful for getting about — although not necessarily for getting to and from walks.

**Taxis** are another way of getting around Corsica. They are very expensive, however, and only economical when shared by a few people. Agree on a price before setting out, and don't be afraid to bargain.

**Coach tours** may appeal to some of you: you will get to see the major tourist sights and routes in comfort, with the minimum effort.

**Timetables** for the buses and trains used for the walks in this book are printed on the back of the touring map; due to space limitations*, we have been unable to include timetables for *all* public transport operating on the island. Remember, too, that no timetable in a book can ever be as up-to-date as one you can obtain from the local tourist offices (bus timetables) or the SNCF railway station nearest your base. So when you arrive on Corsica, *do* call in at the railway and tourist offices, where you can arm yourself not only with timetables, but with all manner of helpful reading material.

One of the nicest things about getting around Corsica is the availability of good maps!

*For the same reason we have not included any town plans, preferring to use the space to describe more walks. If your general guide does not include town plans, these are available from all the local tourist offices.

# ✺ Touring

Hiring a vehicle (car, motorbike, moped) is the only way really to see Corsica. *Do* check your vehicle thoroughly before setting out, and don't take it if you're not happy with it! Verify all the rental and insurance conditions *in English*, and make sure you understand them. Carry the rental firm's *24-hour telephone numbers* with you. If you pay by credit card, check the amount you sign for and keep all receipts!

The touring notes are brief: they include little history or information about the towns; all this is freely available from local *syndicats d'initiative* (tourist information offices). Instead, I've concentrated on the 'logistics' of touring: times and distances, road conditions, and seeing parts of Corsica that most tourists miss. Most of all, I emphasise possibilities for **walking** and **picnicking**.

**Drive carefully**, watching for **oncoming cars** (Corsicans habitually drive in the centre of the road until they see an approaching car), **foraging livestock** (especially on mountain roads), and **cyclists** (who are not obliged by law to travel in single file). There are frequent police checks, so keep to the **speed limits** (110km/h on the few dual carriageways, 90km/h on main roads, 70km/h on other roads — reducing to 50km/h or 30km/h in built-up areas). **Allow enough time**: I have only included brief stops at viewpoints labelled ⌖. Many **petrol stations**, especially inland, will be **closed on Sundays/holidays** … even on Saturday afternoons! Take along warm clothing and some food and drink, and **be prepared for delays** on mountain roads (where passes may be closed in bad weather).

**The large touring map is designed to be held out opposite the touring notes** and contains all the information you need outside the towns. **The tours** (based on Ajaccio, Calvi, Bastia, and Porto-Vecchio) are **numbered in order**

of importance (thus, if your time is limited, 'Calvi 1' would be the most highly recommended tour from Calvi).

The **symbols** used in the text correspond to those in the touring map key. But in the interest of clarity, we have *not* put *all* these symbols on the map itself; hotels, restaurants and petrol stations, for example, only appear on the touring map if they are in an *isolated location*.

# Short walks and picnic suggestions

Corsica is unbeatable for picnicking, with hundreds of natural, unspoiled locations. There are also some 'official' picnic sites with tables, benches and fountains; those on or near the touring routes have been highlighted in the notes and on the touring map with a ⨅.

Several of my favourite picnic spots are near the car tours and are ideal for stretching your legs. These are mentioned at the top of each tour and at the appropriate place in the touring notes. For a full description, turn to the relevant walk (the picnic spot will be highlighted on the *walking* map with the symbol *P*). Unless you can picnic just by your car, remember to wear sensible shoes; if the picnic spot is not in shade, take a sunhat with you. A plastic sheet is a good idea, too, in case the ground is damp or prickly. While some of my short walk/picnic suggestions may not be suitable during a long car tour, you may see a landscape that you would like to explore at leisure another day.

Fill your hamper with the exquisite local cheeses (*brocciu* is a good one), *charcutérie* (try *coppa* and *lonzu*), fresh fruit, *embrocciata* (a cheese tartlet) and of course some wine and *local* spring water (like St-Georges, Zilia, or Orezza).

**All motorists and picnickers should read the Country code on page 52 and go quietly in the countryside. *Bon appetit!***

*The Plage de l'Ostriconi (Walk 20), backed by the hills of the Désert des Agriates. You can picnic on the coastal path, or at the little wooden footbridge that crosses the lagoon (Etang de Foce).*

## Ajaccio 1: THE PINK CLIFFS OF THE PORTO GULF AND THE SPELUNCA GORGE

### Ajaccio • Piana • Porto • Ota • Evisa • Vico • Ajaccio

*Some narrow winding roads are followed on this tour. The D81 between Piana and Porto is very narrow and congested with tour coaches and camper vans, and in some places there are steep, unprotected drops; if you do the tour in the direction I describe, this will be no problem, as you will be on the inland side of the road. Watch out for foraging animals on all inland roads. No petrol stations between Porto and Vico (48km). In early spring and late autumn some mountain passes may be closed. Reckon on 210km/130mi, about 7h driving.*

En route: Walks 2, 10, 11, 13, 14, 15; Walk 1 is nearby. Picnic suggestions for Walks 1, 10, 13, 14

This tour is packed with unsurpassed coastal scenery. The pink cliffs of the Golfe de Porto are by no means overrated, nor are the intriguing crags of les Calanche. The great inland valleys, with their chestnut and oak forests, will entice you back another day — perhaps for a picnic, a debauchery of local food and superb scenery.

Leave Ajaccio on the main north route (N193), following signs for Cargèse/Calvi. Some 6.5km out, just beyond **Mezzavia**, strike off north for Cargèse on the D81. The towering Rocher des Gozzi, shown on page 58, bulges out of the hills on your right, capturing your attention. Walk 2 would take you to the summit, from where there is one of the finest outlooks in the vicinity. Appietto, the starting point for the walk, is signposted at 13km (on your right, but easily missed).

Climbing over the squat hills that block out the Golfe de Sagone, you look down onto verdant fields lining the valley that empties in the tiny Golfu di Lava. Scarlet poppies, violet bugloss, dandelions and indigo vetch turn the roadside into a garden. You cross a saddle, the **Bocca San Bastiano**, and meet with a striking panorama (📷🍴). First you'll see hills stepping their way inland to the 'master peaks' — glimmering

*View from the D81 over the Porto Gulf and Genoese tower*

white beacons, when still capped in snow. Then the Sagone Gulf distracts you, with its exquisite generous bays of white sand and turquoise water. You pass through a trickle of tourist hamlets and the vast untouched beach that sits at the mouth of the Liamone River. **Sagone** (38km ▲▲▲△✕🚐), the junction for Evisa and Vico, follows. Turn left to keep along the coastal D81, which has narrowed considerably by now. Further around the gulf, you look back onto the outstretched arm of the Capo di Feno. Soon you're in **Cargèse** (52km ✝▲▲▲△✕). The village is stepped up a hillside overlooking a cove. This small resort was founded by Greeks, and Roman and Greek Catholic churches face each other in the centre; the latter contains some 17th-century icons.

Your entry into **Piana** (72km ▲▲▲✕🚐) could not be more grand: coming down from the hills, you look straight across the majestic **Porto Gulf**★ (📷), perhaps the most beautiful in the whole of Europe. This natural harbour of pink granite cliffs rising out of an intensely blue sea is spellbinding. Small green coves sit back in the cliffs. And Piana, perched high above the sea, soaks up this unparalleled panorama. Let's do some exploring. On coming into the village, drive past the first hotel. Then fork left on a lane, to the **Saliccio Belvedere**★ (📷). From this viewing point you look out onto the mountainous

*Ota, with the cloven peak of the Capu d'Orto (Walk 15) and the higher Capu di u Vitullu in the background*

interior and over the weird rock formations of les Calanche. Hidden in the sheer cliffs below is the tiny cove of Ficajola and, if you drive down to it, you will have a splendid view into the Calanche: return to the D81 and turn off left just before the church (signposted 'Plage d'Arone'). One kilometre along, take the first turning right and zigzag down a *very narrow road* to **Ficajola★**, from where a path drops you down into this memorable cove. Prefer beach swimming? Return to the turn-off and continue some 10km further, towards the Plage d'Arone. This exhilarating drive carries you past **Capo Rosso★**, a mountain of rock hanging off the southern arm of the gulf, adorned by a Genoese watchtower. When the road forks, keep left to the **Plage d'Arone** (91km).

From the Plage d'Arone, return to Piana and continue north on the D81. About 1km outside Piana you cross the Pont de Mezzanu *(not signposted),* where Walks 14 and 15 begin. You're now winding through the pink world of **les Calanche★** (📷). Guy de Maupassant described it as a 'forest of purple granite'. Walks 13-15 explore les Calanche in depth. Why not try either Walk 14 (which begins here at the Pont de Mezzanu) or Walk 13, which begins 5.5km further north, at the signposted Tête de Chien? Both are ideal leg-stretchers.

Out of this 'jungle' of rock, you pass some pine-shaded picnic spots (no facilities except rubbish bins). The gulf reappears, and Porto comes into view. It sits in a poster-like setting★, best appreciated from above: the rich colour contrasts of the pale-grey pebble beach, blue sea, green vegetation and rose-coloured rock shoreline are a rare sight. **Porto** (114km 🏨 ⛺ ▲ ✕ ☕ 📷), built solely for tourism, is overlooked by a square Genoese watchtower. Continuing past the village, turn inland, swinging sharply back to the right on the D124 towards Ota. Ascending into the deep Porto Valley, you come into olive trees. Spring-green chestnut groves stand out in the dark cloak of the surrounding vegetation.

**Ota** (119km 🏔🏠✖️📷; Walks 10 and 11) is an impressive sight. The village, shown opposite and on page 76, is perched high on the hillside amidst olive trees. Pink craggy walls tower overhead. Bump your way down to the **Ponte Vecchiu★** (📷), the beautifully-restored Genoese foot-bridge seen ahead. This is a perfect picnic spot, where you can take an invigorating swim ... but expect company — it's in all the guides. A minute later you cross 'les Deux Ponts d'Ota', two enchanting stone bridges at the confluence of the Onca River and the **Gorges de Spelunca★**. A path on the left, just beyond the second bridge, would take you up the gorge to another lovely picnic spot in 30 minutes — the Genoese Pont de Zaglia (see Short walk 10, page 73; photograph page 74).

From here we climb to a junction and turn *very sharply* left on the D84 for Evisa. The road swings back into another gorge full of chestnut groves. At the sign denoting the entrance to **Evisa** (137km 🏔🏠△✖️), a viewpoint on the left (📷) gives you a last opportunity to capture all this beauty with a photograph. Walk 10 begins here.

Turn sharp right on the D70 at the junction beyond Evisa. From the **Col de Sevi** (1101m/3610ft 📷), you enjoy a fine view back over the Tavulella Valley. On the descent, an immense valley (the Gorges de Liamone) opens up on your left, dominated by the Punta di a Spusata. Turn left into **Vico** (159km 🏔△✖️🚏). A few hundred metres from the junction, turn right for the Couvent de St-François (✝). A wood-carving of Christ in the 15th-century church is claimed to be the oldest on Corsica. Vico is a village full of character, with tall granite buildings lining its alleys and single main street.

To complete the circuit, return to the D70 and follow it back to Sagone. You drop down through wooded hills to the Sagone Valley floor. Lush pastures fill the river flat. Alders trickle along the stream banks. In May the fields are flooded with deep blue *Echium* — a dazzling sight. From Sagone, head left on the D81 to **Ajaccio** (210km).

*Walk 13 begins at the 'Dog's Head' (Tête de Chien) on the D81 and takes you past spectacular rock formations (see photograph page 78)*

# Ajaccio 2: COUNTRY ROADS TO BASTELICA

## Ajaccio • Porticcio • Coti-Chiavari • Bastelica • Gorges du Prunelli • Tolla • Ajaccio

*The roads are variable, generally narrow and winding. The stretches between Marato and the Col St-Georges and Bastelica and Tolla are **exceptionally narrow**; some people will find them vertiginous. Be alert for foraging animals on inland roads. No petrol stations between Porticcio and Bastelicaccia (117km). Reckon on 174km/108mi, 7h driving.*

En route: Walks 1, 3 (both with short walk and picnic suggestions)

G et out into the countryside and savour rural Corsica, an island where much of the land remains untamed, covered in maquis and a wealth of forests. In springtime you will be overwhelmed by the extravaganza of wild flowers illuminating the hills. The highlight of this tour is the jade-green Tolla Reservoir. But don't be too late returning to Ajaccio for the fire of pink sunset over the Iles Sanguinaires!

Follow the N196 (main south road) out to the Porticcio junction (11.5km) and turn off on the D55 to **Porticcio** (17.5km ▲▲▲△✕☐WC), one of Corsica's largest tourist centres. Its beautiful golden beach and picturesque setting are now the casualties of development. Much of this side of the gulf is 'ritzy-residential'. Following the coast, you curve in and out of pretty bays and coves. Your view extends across the harbour to Ajaccio and the hills behind it.

Approaching Verghia, you skirt the most beautiful beach on this stretch of coast. The long white sand collar curves round towards a stand of pines. If you would like to see the beautiful cork oak wood shown opposite (and, in spring, a deluge of wild flowers) try the short version of Walk 3 and go up into the Forêt Domaniale de Chiavari. This signposted nature trail (Sentier du Myrte) is near the end of the beach (28km), immediately before the bridge over the Ruisseau de Zirione. (The longer version of Walk 3 begins on the far side of the same bridge.)

The main tour continues on the D55, which turns off left less than 1km further on, in **Verghia** (29km ▲▲△✕). Now you climb through a magnificent evergreen forest to **Coti-Chiavari** (39km ▲▲✕☞). This small terraced village sits at the foot of a maquis wood, with a fine outlook over the tail of the gulf to the Iles Sanguinaires. Descending from the settlement, you look down onto another tower-crowned headland, the Capu di Muru. Just over 5km beyond Coti-Chiavari, pass the turn-off for the Capu di Muru and bear left.

Splendid coastal views follow you all the way, as you

14

head east over the hills. In the distance, ridges pour down off the island's central spine. Below lies the deeply-indented Baie de Cupabia, with an irresistible, untouched beach. If you're ready for a break, this bay may be just what you're looking for: the turn-off comes up on your right after 53km. The main tour keeps left here towards Serra-di-Ferro, then turns left and left again, on the D355 for Tassinca and the Col de Gradello.

You climb into the hills, where goats roam wild. Meet the D55 again, and turn right. Not far beyond **Marato**, the only village out here in 'the wilds', be sure to take the *second* right-hand turn to continue on the D55 (sign-

*These lovely cork oaks on the Sentier du Myrte (Short walk 3 and Picnic suggestion) can only be stripped every 10-12 years.*

posted for Sta-Maria-Siché). Hugging steep rocky hill-sides on an exceptionally narrow road lined with dazzling yellow *Coronilla,* you look out over a wooded valley. Keep left all the way to the N196, then turn left, to climb to the **Col St-Georges** (84km ▲✕▣).

Descend from the pass (⊼) and come to the outskirts of Cauro (▲▲✕). Turn sharp right on the D27 before entering the village. You meander along a lush valley occupied by small farms and boskets. Soon you disappear into the high hills again and, 4km before you reach Bastelica, you pass by the turn-off left to Tolla (your return route). Perhaps what you'll remember most about **Bastelica** (109.5km ▲▲▲✕) is the magnificent chestnut wood that surrounds it. Your approach to the village takes you past tired old stone walls that enclose plots and orchards. Some fine old stone mansions are found in the six hamlets that comprise Bastelica, stretching out across the valley inclines. Drive between the houses, keeping straight on at the church, then swing back left beyond the church to return to the Tolla turn-off. Monte Renoso (Corsica's fourth highest peak at 2352m/7715ft) sits high in the valley.

Turn right when you reach the Tolla road (D3), a *very* narrow route cut into the gorge walls. Your homeward route follows the scenic **Gorges du Prunelli★**, a continuation of Bastelica's picturesque valley. Drive *very carefully* and only admire the views where you can pull over off the road *safely*. The river flows far below. Rounding a corner, the gorge opens up, and the jade-green **Lac de Tolla★** (a reservoir) fills the valley floor. What a view! A collar of pink rock, marking the waterline, separates the sherwood green of the wooded hillsides from the jade-green of the lake. **Tolla** (115.5km ✕▣) is the village set high on the grassy slopes, overlooking both the dam and the rugged interior. Beyond the village, a lay-by enables you to pull off the road and enjoy the setting (▣). Crossing the **Bocca di Mercujo** (✕), park at the restaurant and follow the track to the belvedere★ (▣ 10min downhill) for a more spectacular view of the dam and gorge.

Follow the D3 back to the N196 just beyond **Bastelicaccia** and turn right, back to **Ajaccio** (174km). To see the magnificent sunset over the Iles Sanguinaires, go straight through town and follow the coast out to the **Pointe de la Parata**, 12km west (✕▣; Walk 1 and Picnic suggestion). Find yourself a soft piece of ground and let it all take place...

# Ajaccio 3: SOME HISTORY ... AND THE D69

**Ajaccio • Col St-Georges • Filitosa • Propriano • Campomoro • Sartène • Aullène • Zicavo • Santa-Maria-Siché • Ajaccio**

*This is a long and tiring tour, which is best divided into two days — the western side one day and the scenic D69 another. The country roads and the D69 are very narrow and bumpy. All roads are winding; driving will be slow. Watch out for foraging animals. Motorcyclists and moped riders should carry extra fuel; some of the rural petrol stations don't have the mixture for mopeds. Reckon on 250km/155mi, 10h driving.*

En route: No walks or picnic suggestions

This drive is brim-full of magnificent country scenery and at its best in spring, when the meadows are saturated with wild flowers and the trees are freshly green. You dip in and out of gentle farmed valleys interrupted by rocky hills. But as usual, it's the mountain landscape that lures you on: the cosy, welcoming perched villages, the vast woodlands cloaking the slopes, and the far-reaching views as you climb higher and higher, up to where the shepherds graze their flocks. Also en route lie Filitosa and Sartène, two very different glimpses of Corsica's turbulent history — a prehistoric site and a town that clings to tradition.

Leave Ajaccio by heading south on the main N196 towards Propriano. You cross the Prunelli River and climb to the **Col St-Georges** (29km ▲✕🖾). Once over the pass, you look out over an enormous basin of low rolling valleys. Silvery-green olive trees stand out amid evergreen oaks. Cross the Taravo River and soon the woods give way to fields. Pass through **Casalabriva** (57km ▲▲✕), then, 1.8km further on, leave the N196: turn sharp right on a narrow country road to **Sollacaro**, an appealing, rustic village steeped in history. Literature buffs may be interested to know that Dumas' novel, *The Corsican Brothers* (which incidentally has little to do with the island), came out of his short sojourn here in 1841.

*Sartène*

Boswell also spent some time here in 1765, in the company of Pasquale Paoli, the first and only president of an independent Corsica (1755-68. Just through Sollacaro turn sharp left on the D57, down to an undulating plain spread out along the Taravo delta.

If you're not 'into' history, you won't find the insubstantial **Station Préhistorique de Filitosa★** (68km ⬛🏠 ✕M) overly exciting. However, compensation enough for nature lovers is the site's picturesque setting and the profusion of wild flowers in spring, especially the clusters of purple orchids. Filitosa is the island's most important prehistoric settlement and amazingly, this site remained undetected for nearly 5000 years. An avenue of pines leads you to the *menhirs* (stone-carved megalithic 'statues' that resemble standing mummies). Cork and olive trees beautify the site, and cows graze nearby. If you read French, you'll find the small museum here of interest.

Following the Taravo, you head towards a coastline sprinkled with holiday homes and tourist hamlets. Your view extends across the Golfe de Valinco to a long inviting stretch of sand at the foot of the Taravo hills — the Plage de Portigliolo. This will be your 'beach stop' later in the tour. Propriano is just across the bay now. Unfortunately, the terminal disease of tourism is already beginning to eat away at the setting. Some 5km before the town, you rejoin the N196 and circle behind the beach at **Propriano** (86.5km ⬛🏠▲△✕🏪⊕). You can either visit the town or bypass it by following signs for Porto-Vecchio. Just beyond the Rizzanèse River, leave the N196 and turn right on the D121, towards the coast. Passing Propriano's Tavaria Aerodrome, the road skirts the superb Plage de Portigliolo, the long beach that you could see from across the bay. A low ridge of sand rises off the aquamarine sea and folds over into green fields. You can park at the end of the beach.

Crossing the hills for Campomoro, you get a stunning panorama over this clear sweeping bay and onto the distant encircling hills. Shortly, the tiny village of **Belvédère** is reached. Perfectly named, this hillside perch has an enviable view (📷) straight out over the harbour. From here continue to **Campomoro** (102km 🏁⬛▲△✕), a seaside village set around a shallow beach. A Genoese tower adorns a nearby promontory. Settlement on the maquis-covered hillsides is slowly eroding Campomoro's 'off-the-beaten-track' appeal.

Return to Belvédère and continue straight ahead,

along the D221. You enter an isolated (not to say bleak) countryside drenched in scrub. Bypass Grossa, a handful of stone houses set back off the road. Further on, you circle some farms well ensconced in these wavy hills. The landscape is beautifully untamed, rocky and woven in maquis. Put your head out of the car window and smell the fragrance — a mixture of cistus, lavender and thorny broom. The D21 carries you to a T-junction with the D48. Tizzano (and the prehistoric sites of Cauria and Palaggiu) are to the right. Personally, I found Tizzano (□ ▲▲ ✕) over-rated in many guides, and the main tour doesn't visit it. But both sites are signposted, if you wish to take a detour.

Turn left on the D48 and left again on meeting the N196. Mounting a crest, you come to an excellent pano-rama over the Rizzanèse Valley's basin of trees and fields. The town of **Sartène ★** (127km ♦ ▲▲ ▲ △ ✕ 🅿 ⊕ M) terraces a steep hillside. Coming into town, you pass the imposing San Damiano Monastery (♦) and look over a hillside forti-fied with tall stone buildings. Sartène terraces a steep hill-side. It is one of Corsica's most traditional towns, where matters of honour and the vendetta were much in evi-dence for longer then anywhere else on the island. The place is now best known for its Good Friday 'Procession du Castenacciu', a three hour-long parade of hooded penitents through candle-lit streets, which harks back to medieval times. Climb the steps and wander through the back streets and alleys, sampling the delights of this living history book. The museum of Corsican pre-history houses a wide collection of objects dating back to 6000BC (of particular interest if you visit any sites on this tour). The tree-shaded Place de la Libération is at the heart of the town: here are the town hall (formerly the palace of the Genoese governor) and the 18th-century Eglise Ste-Marie.

If the day hasn't passed you by, from Sartène make for the D69: follow the N196 towards Ajaccio and turn right on the D268 for Ste-Lucie-de-Tallano. But don't forget to look back on Sartène! Just over 4km along, look out left for the arched **Spin'a Cavallu ★** (the 'Horse's Back'; 📷 🏕), a beautifully restored 13th-century Genoese bridge (*not signposted;* parking opposite). Heading inland, you pass pastures knee-high in grass and speckled with red, purple and yellow flowers. On reaching the first junction, turn left on the D69 for Aullène, crossing the Rizzanèse.

An intriguing countryside opens up before you. The Rizzanèse twists its way through the central massif. A few lone houses enjoy the solitude of this cut-off valley. Small

*Cascade on the D69 outside Zicavo*

stone bridges and the ever-present wild flowers add to the countryfied charm. At a T-junction, turn left (still on the D69) for **Aullène** (163km ▲▲ ✕🖺). Set amidst chestnut groves and silhouetted against a cone-shaped mountain, this village curves around the crest of a ridge.

From Aullène follow signs for Zicavo. Leaving the trees behind, you climb into cow-herds' domain — a bleak, rocky landscape with meagre pastureland scattered amongst the heather-clad slopes. Humble farm dwellings have been converted into attractive summer retreats. Crossing a pass, the **Col de la Vaccia** (📷), you have a wonderful view back across this elevated valley onto Aullène, comfortably set in the woodlands below. To the west lies the deep Taravo Valley and, all around you, a choppy sea of hills and mountains. Descending, you come into splendid beech woods; under the evening sun the leaves glow and the hills come alight. Around here, be sure to search the roadside for exquisite mountain anemones. Their colour varies from off-white or pale mauve to blue. You may also spot clumps of almost-fluorescent pale-green hellebores.

You cross over the roaring cascade shown above just before entering **Zicavo** (189km ▲▲✕). Turn left as you come into the top of the village. A narrow wooded gorge leads you out of this enclosed valley, and you briefly follow the Taravo River once more. At the junction 4km downhill, turn sharp left for Ajaccio. Some 2.4km further on, as you pass through the pretty tree-lined village of **Bains de Guitera** (▲▲✕🖺), fork right on the D83 (195km).

Climbing up through forested valleys, you cross yet another pass. Rustic, shuttered villages, all picturesquely located, lie along your homeward route: some cling to ridges, some adorn prominent crags, and some shelter in hollows. A couple of kilometres before rejoining the N196, you come to the farming village of **Sta-Maria-Siché** (216km 🛏▲▲✕🖺). Watch for the 15th-century Château d'Ornano, set in the trees just below the village. Once back on the N196, turn right: a straight run of 34km takes you to **Ajaccio** (250km).

# Calvi 1: THE ISOLATED NIOLO BASIN AND THE BREATH-TAKING WESTERN GULFS

## Calvi • l'Ile-Rousse • Ponte Leccia • Col de Vergio • Evisa • Gorges de Spelunca • Ota • Calvi

*Beyond Ponte Leccia driving will be slow: the route is winding and often narrow. Always be on the alert for foraging animals! The weather can be cold and cloudy (much of the route is quite high); the Col de Vergio may be closed in bad weather. There are no petrol stations between l'Ile-Rousse and Ponte Leccia (41km) or Calacuccia and Porto (51km). Since this is such a long drive, I have omitted les Calanche; allow another full day for exploring the environs of the Porto Gulf (use the notes for 'Ajaccio 1'). I highly recommend doing this tour in the direction described (especially if you have nervous passengers), due to the narrow roads beyond Porto. Reckon on 237km/147mi, about 7h30min driving.*

En route: Walks 10, 11, 12, 16, 17, 18, 19, 20; Walks 24, 25 and 26 are nearby. Picnic suggestions for Walks 10, 12, 17, 18, 20 and 24

Crossing the island's central spine of mountains, you pass through the isolated Niolo Basin, home of shepherds and herdsmen. On your return to the west coast, you climb to the Col de Vergio, the highest road pass on Corsica (1477m). You can cool off in the fresh limpid pools of the Aitone or Spelunca gorges, before descending to the beautiful gulfs of Porto and Girolata.

From Calvi take the N197 (the main north road for l'Ile-Rousse and Bastia). Crossing the plain, you look up to the pretty hillside village of Lumio★ (9.5km ⚑🏔🏔▲△✕✕; photograph page 31), terracing the hills of Capu d'Occi and Capu Bracajo. It commands a fine view over the Calvi Gulf and the citadel. Pass 'Chez Charles' (where Walk 18 ends and Alternative walk 18 begins) and, at the junction, keep left on the N197 to continue along the coast. You look down onto Marine de Sant' Ambrogio (🏔🏔▲✕), a classy resort. Pass above Algajola (16km □⚑🏔🏔▲△✕🏳), another major resort, at the end of a curving bay. Its Genoese fort is in ruins, except for the citadel. Inland, Monte Grosso dominates the great wall of mountains.

You pass several roads leading inland to the Balagne (Car tour 'Calvi 3'). Then, just before l'Ile-Rousse, you pass the striking (and least spoilt) beach along this stretch of coast, the Plage de Botre, sitting off the turquoise-blue Baie de Guinchetu. All you see of **l'Ile-Rousse** (23km ⚑🏔🏔 ▲△✕🏳⊕🗺WC) is a street lined with plane trees. Save your visit to this very pleasant town (photographs pages 31 and 91) for the day you do Walk 19, which ends here.

Further along the coast your views extend to the more rugged shore line of the Désert des Agriates and, in the distance, Cap Corse. Beyond the entrance to the **Parc de Saleccia** (27km ✿), you skirt the extensive sandy beach of **Lozari** (30km) and keep along the wide coastal road (now the N1197, 'la Balanina'). The road swings inland above the lovely landscape shown on pages 8-9 — the unspoilt Plage de l'Ostriconi (Walk 20). At the next junction, ignore the D81 left to St-Florent and Bastia; keep along the Ostriconi Valley on the N1197 for Ponte Leccia.

At **Ponte Leccia** (67km ▲▲▲△✕🛏), a major junction, you join the N193. Carry on past **Francardo** (off to the right at 76km; ▲▲✕) and, just after crossing the Golo, turn right on the D84 for Calacuccia. The Golo, Corsica's great 84km-long river, runs along on your right. Recrossing the river after 6km, bear left. You enter a magnificent gorge, the **Scala di Sta Regina★**, a winding passageway that links the Niolo with the east. Rocky hillsides tumble off the towering mountain chain that rises some 1000m/3300ft on either side. Approaching the **Niolo★**, the gorge opens out, and rough pastures appear. Remains of stone walls, footbridges, and solitary huts speak of grazing land.

Just before you enter Calacuccia, fork left on the D218 towards Casamaccioli and circle the picturesque **Barrage de Calacuccia**. You cross the dam wall and look over the reservoir to the amphitheatre of rocky mountains that encloses this high basin. Sloping pastures lie between the scattering of sheltered hamlets and the crags. Monte Cinto (Corsica's highest peak at 2706m/8875ft) stands out with its ramp-shaped summit. **Casamaccioli** (100km 🛐▲) is a pretty village set back off the wooded banks of the lake. Every year on the 8th of September, the island's most important festival is held here (the Nativity of the Virgin). All the shepherds return from the mountains with their flocks for this three-day fête; if you're in the area, don't miss it!

At the T-junction just inside Casamaccioli, turn right and continue around the lake, a lovely place to picnic. Returning to **Calacuccia** (105km 🛐▲▲✕🛏), turn left and drive through it. The village is quite ordinary, but superbly sited overlooking the lake. In the church there is an interesting 17th-century wooden statue of Christ; the carving is particularly expressive. Continuing on the D84, you pass below a 17th-century Franciscan monastery (🛐) set back in the trees. Beyond **Albertacce** (107km ▲▲ and **M** of archaeology) you cross the Golo for the last time (📷). Note the small footbridge below left and the pretty gorge cutting back up to the right.

As you head across the plateau, the landscape becomes noticeably rocky and is clad in trees and bushes. Soon pines take over, and you're in the **Forêt de Valdu**

**Niellu★**, Corsica's largest forest (🏕). Some of these pencil-straight trees reach a height of 50m/165ft. Pull over at a roadside viewpoint (📷), to look back down the bowl-shaped Golo Valley to the dam. Still climbing, come to the ski station and the highest hotel on the island (🏨✕). Approaching the **Col de Vergio★** (📷; 1477m/ 4845ft), you catch a glimpse of the Punta Licciola and, behind it, the 'pierced' summit of Capu Tafunatu — one of the focal points on Walk 25 (photograph page 102). From the pass there are more splendid views towards the Licciola peak and other bare summits, all lightly flecked

*Brightly-blooming hillsides: late spring in the Niolo*

with a luminous green lichen, and down over the Golo. The Col de Vergio straddles the island's north/south border (Haute-Corse and Corse-du-Sud), two very different and mutually antagonistic cultures. The statue of Christ here, with its reconciliatory subtext, 'Love one another as I have loved you', was the inspiration of Evisa's priest.

Over the pass, the Aitone Valley winds its way seaward. The **Cascades d'Aitone★** (⊓), 7.5km down from the pass, make a good cooling-off stop, so *watch carefully* for a track off right to the Aitone Forestry House and park immediately below it (Walk 12; picnic suggestion).

Out of the forest, you enter chestnut groves. Turn right at the junction and head for **Evisa** (133km ▲▲▲△✕), a charming mountain village, well placed for exploring the interior and the Porto Gulf area. Walk 10 sets out from here. At the village exit, a signpost, 'Spelunca' alerts you to a roadside balcony on the right (🖎) with a splendid view of Ota, perched high in the deep Porto Valley. The rocky hillsides here blush pink, and pinnacles of rock burst up out of the surrounding walls. The road curls down into a side valley thick with chestnut trees. Keep right past two turn-offs left for Marignana ; then, 14km from Evisa, be prepared for a *very sharp right turn* onto the single-lane D124 for Ota. You soon cross the Porto River, at the mouth of the **Gorges de Spelunca★**. There are two good picnicking choices here, both by Genoese foot-bridges: see the Short walk/picnic suggestion on page 73 and photographs on page 74. A few hundred metres beyond 'les Deux Ponts d'Ota' ('Ota's Two Bridges', where there is usually enough room to park), you look down onto the lovely, high-arched **Ponte Vecchiu★** (🖎), one of the suggested picnic settings. The river here is ideal for swimming.

This narrow road has carried us to **Ota** (148km ▲▲▲✕ 🖎), the colourful village with bright orange-tiled rooftops shown on pages 12 and 76. A lofty ridge capped in rose-coloured rock looms above it. Walk 10 ends here, and Walk 11 begins here. Leaving the valley, you come down to the tourist village of Porto (Tour 'Ajaccio 1'). This tour doesn't enter Porto; instead, turn right at the junction, on the D81. From here you have the superb **view of Porto★** and its spectacular setting shown on pages 10-11. The rock dome of the Capu d'Orto, behind you, stands guard over the bay. Superb seascapes open up over the headlands. Twin-headed Monte Seninu rises straight up out of the sea, dramatically punctuating the end of the gulf. A vast beach, the Plage de Bussaglia (🛆🛆🛆🛆✕), appears below. Watch for the lovely fountain shown on page 2 near the turning right to Serriera. Beautiful eucalyptus trees line the way to **Partinello** (with a similar fountain at the end of the village).

Continue along the corniche to the **Bocca di a Croce**★ (✕). Pull over to the parking area *carefully* (dangerous bend) and continue on foot to the viewpoint (📷). The pretty cove of Girolata sits tucked back in a striking stretch of coast. Shorter walk 26 *(highly recommended)* leads from this pass to Girolata via the Anse de Tuara, an exquisite cove (notes page 103; photograph page 104).

Some 12km further on you cross the **Col de Palmarella**; the road widens and descends into the flat-bottomed Fango Valley (🅿). This is the setting for Short walk 24 so, when you tire of beaches, one day take the D351 up into this peaceful valley, find yourself your own rock pool, and enjoy a lazy day of swimming, sunning and picnicking. This unbelievably lovely setting, with a riverbed ranging in colour from pink to purple, and blue and green river pools, is a particular favourite of mine (see Short walk/ picnic suggestion on page 98; photos on pages 98,100).

Turn left down the valley, then right for Calvi. But first, if you have time, continue on the D351 towards Galéria (🗋🛆🛆🛆🛆✕ and start of Walk 26). You pass a good tourist information kiosk on your left. Park on the right after 3km, just below the tower. Then walk down to the enticing beach at the mouth of the Fango, a UNESCO protected area, with its pretty lagoon and enchanting coppice.

The main tour continues on the D81 by crossing the Fango. At the junction, turn left along the longer and *narrower,* but far prettier coastal route (D81b), with fine views back over the Golfe de Galéria. Coming into **l'Argentella** (214km 🛆🛆🛆✕), you look out over the Baie de Crovani. L'Argentella sits on the edge of an open valley, sheltered by a sweeping curve of rocky hills. Back along the coast, your views reach to la Revellata, the arm of land with the lighthouse (Walk 16; photograph page 83). Having rounded the turquoise-green Baie de Nichia-reto, you enjoy an amazing vista of fat rocky mountains in shades of pink, orange and grey. Looking out over the jagged sea cliffs serrating the coastline, you pass the turn-off to the chapel of Notre Dame de la Serra★ (✝📷; photographs page 85), one of the settings for Walks 16 and 17 — a delightful place for an evening picnic under a lowering sun. Now **Calvi** is just 4km away (237km)

# Calvi 2: THE ASCO VALLEY

## Calvi • l'Ile-Rousse • Haut Asco • Asco • Calvi

*The road is good as far as the Asco turn-off, but the D147 to Asco narrows to only one lane in places. You may not be able to get as far as Haut Asco in early spring or late autumn. It can also be very cold and misty on this high road. Watch for foraging animals. Ponte Leccia, 2km beyond the Asco turn-off, is your last chance for petrol for 62km. Reckon on 192km/119mi, 6h driving.*

En route: Walks 18, 19, 20. Picnic suggestions for Walks 18 and 20

The Asco Valley is one of those gorges that disappears into the interior mountains and then stops dead in its tracks at the foot of towering crags. Paths to attract the curious and energetic abound here, so take a picnic lunch and spend an hour or two somewhere on the edge of the beautiful river that keeps you company all the way up. Then, before the sun has lost its warmth, head back to the Genoese bridge below Asco and revive yourself in the blue-green pool that it spans. Shake the ice off and make for Calvi under a dying sun.

Follow the notes for Car tour 'Calvi 1' all the way to the turn-off for the **Gorges de l'Asco ★** (65km; 2km north of Ponte Leccia). Turn right (D47) and, 5km further on, keep left on the D147 (where the D47 heads off high to Moltifao). Soon great salients of rock loom above. Further along, the abruptness subsides, and the walls lean back to reveal side valleys. Asco (82km) soon comes into sight, built on terraces in the steep valley wall. Without entering the village, swing up right towards the ski station. You come into a magnificent pine forest, the Forêt de Carozzica, as you skirt the gushing Stranciacone River (many good picnic spots and room to park).

**Haut Asco** (93km ⛺▲✕), the ski station, is a bit of an eyesore, but the surrounding alpine scenery is enchanting. It's best to scramble up the slopes until the hotel is out of sight! A breathtaking 30-minute climb would take you past grand Corsican pines and

*Right: pastoral landscape in the Asco Valley*

26

*Calvi's citadel under a setting sun*

up to a plateau strewn with pink and mauve rock, amongst the foothills of **Monte Cinto ★**.

If you fancy a dip in the pool below Asco on your return, take the first right over the bridge and then go right again, to zigzag down a potholed lane to the bridge (swimming is officially banned here, but no one takes any notice). Visit **Asco**, a village dating from the 11th century, then return to **Calvi** the same way (192km). Or try the 'roller-coaster' D47 via Moltifao and, at the T-junction, turn left on the D547, to cross the Capanna Pass and descend to the N197.

## Calvi 3: VILLAGES OF THE BALAGNE, AND THE TARTAGINE VALLEY

### Calvi • Calenzana • Muro • Speloncato • Bocca di a Battaglia • Tartagine Valley • Belgodère • l'Ile-Rousse • Corbara • Sant' Antonino • Lumio • Calvi

*Most of the tour follows narrow, winding roads. Watch out for foraging animals, especially between Speloncato and Belgodère. There are no petrol stations between Cateri and l'Ile-Rousse (98km). The Bocca di a Battaglia might be closed in early spring or late autumn in bad weather. Reckon on 161km/100mi; 6h driving.*

En route: Walks 18, 19, 21; Walks 22-24 are accessible from Calenzana via the D51, but are best reached via the airport road (D81) and then the D251 direct to Bonifatu. Picnic suggestions for Walks 18, 19, 22

The Balagne is a region full of charming villages. Every one seems to have its own baroque church, and all have a balcony view over the plains and hills that characterise the area. Stopping at all of them is impossible, and choosing between them a difficult task. I'll leave that to you. Over the hills, behind this salubrious countryside, lies a quiet, cut-off valley that few people visit, the Tartagine. Its beautiful pine and evergreen oak forests, and the finely-etched Monte Padro, make another lovely circuit, before you return through the Balagne to Calvi.

Follow the Ile-Rousse road (N197) out of Calvi for 4.5km, then turn right on the D151 to **Calenzana** (12.5km ✝🏔⛪🏕✕🍴). Set in a flat valley amidst olive and almond trees, with its back to the prominent Monte Grosso (1938m/6355ft), Calenzana verges on being a town, with its maze of alleys, gardens and shops. It's an important agricultural centre, noted for ewes'-milk cheese *(brocciu)*, wine, and *charcutérie*. The 17th/18th-century baroque church of St-Blaise, shown on page 94, dwarfs the village

*Speloncato from the D63 to Olmi-Cappela*

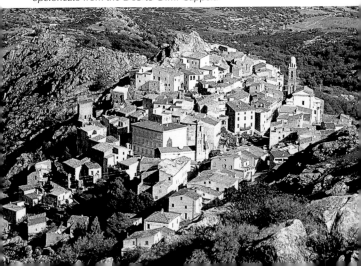

*Sant' Antonino — masterpiece of the Balagne*

centre; its elegant campanile enhances the square. Walk 21 begins here. Just over 1km outside the village, still on the D151, is the tiny church dedicated to Ste-Restitude (✝), a Corsican martyr beheaded by the Romans in 303.

The road winds deeper into the Fiume Seccu Valley, through untidy countryside crammed with olive, oak, cherry and chestnut trees. Barely 7km from Calenzana, you cross a bridge (⌒ by a stream to the right). An enchanting old stone church stands above the road in **Lunghignano** (22km ✝✕). **Montemaggiore** (23.5km ✝🞑) adorns a prominent rocky ridge jutting out into the Fiume Seccu. It commands a fine view over Calvi's gulf. A kilometre out of the village, just where the D151 swings up left, take the dirt track off right, to the simple 12th-century Romanesque church of St-Rainer (✝), resting in fields. Back on the main road and climbing into cistus-covered hills, you have expansive views over the settings for Walks 16 and 17: the plains below, the Calvi Gulf, la Revellata, and the hills of rock that enclose the Figarella Valley. Then, crossing the **Bocca di Salvi ★** (🞑), you look down into the Algajola basin, chequered with fields. Sant' Antonino is perched high on the crest of a ridge ahead.

On meeting an intersection (🚏), turn right on the D71 for Muro. The sickle-shaped Codole Reservoir stretches out in the floor of the Regino Valley. After 4km, turn right into **Muro** (33km ✝✕🞑); you arrive at the door of the imposing church, the Eglise de l'Annonciation, one of the finest examples of the baroque style on Corsica. Continue past the church to leave Muro and turn right again on the D71. **Feliceto** (39km ▲▲✕) is surrounded by orchards. Leave the D71 when the way forks and turn right (D663) for **Speloncato** (45km ✝▲▲▲✕🖼️), strategically sited on a high outcrop of rock overlooking the Regino basin.

From here you ascend for some fine views over **the Balagne★**. Squeezing through the narrow streets, take the narrow Olmi-Cappela road (D63) out of Speloncato. Climb past a derelict monastery and the view shown on page 28 to the **Bocca di a Battaglia★** (🖼️🏠). Here an even more stupendous panorama unfolds — over the reservoir, Speloncato, the embroidery of fields in the Regino Valley, the luminous green Lozari Bay, the arid Désert des Agriates, Cap Corse, and the red Ile-Rousse.

You drop down into a tree-flooded valley. On reaching the D963, turn sharp right, then keep right for the rest of the way. The bumpy road winds high above the Melaja and **Tartagine★** valleys. Monte Padro (2390m/7840ft) dominates the landscape on your left. Beyond a shuttered forestry house, you cross the Tartagine, a healthy stream with knee-deep pools. The road ends at private property (parking area), but enticing paths lead into the forest.

Turn back along the D963 and continue straight through Olmi-Cappela, to join the N197. Turn left for l'Ile-Rousse and pass above Palasca, a lonely village nestled round its church. You might like to visit the imposing 13th-century Church of St-Thomas at **Belgodère** (112km ▢✝✕ 🖼️WC), another strategically-sited village. From the scant remains of the fortress that once dominated the settlement, you look down over the Regino and Prato valleys. Circling down above the fertile plains, you pass the turn-off to Regino and Lozari's tempting beach. Head straight through **l'Ile-Rousse** (128km ✝▲▲▲△✕🗠 🖼️WC); it deserves a visit, but is easily accessible by train from Calvi. Walk 19 ends here. Some 1.5km out of town, bear right (signposted 'Calvi') and then go left immediately on the D151 for Corbara. From the hillside, the Baie de Guinchetu and the Plage de Botre look enticing. Turn left again at the next fork (for clarity, refer to the large-scale map on pages 88-89).

From the instant you see **Corbara** (132km ✝✕🖼️WC), you know it's going to be different. Palm trees in a garden above the road set the scene. There's a distinct Moorish flavour about the place. From the chapel of Notre Dame (built into the rocky vertex above the village and once the site of the Castel de Corbara), you have fine views over Algajola Bay to la Revellata. The 18th-century Church of the Annunciation stands guard over the village.

Continuing round the Algajola basin, with good views

Left: churches in Lumio (top) and Aregno; right: l'Ile-Rousse

of Corbara's setting, you pass a row of magnificent family tombs on the right and soon spot the imposing 15th-century Monastery of Corbara★ (✝) below Monte Sant' Angelo. **Pigna** (134km) crowns a hillock growing out of the valley wall. The village is a handicraft centre★, where traditional arts such as weaving, pottery, and wood-working are practised. A profusion of olive and citrus trees welcomes you to **Aregno** (137km ✝). Stop at one of the area's masterpieces, the 12th-century Pisan Romanesque Eglise de la Trinité★ (on the D151), to see the humorous figurines decorating the façade and two exquisite 15th-century frescoes. Then, just 1km beyond Aregno, *turn sharp left* (D413) for the 'pièce de résistance' of the Balagne, **Sant' Antonino**★ (141km ✕🖼), where Walk 19 begins. This 9th-century settlement is a treasure-trove of old and restored buildings (see page 90 for picnic suggestions).

Returning to the D151, head left and, at the junction 500m along, turn right towards Lumio. **Cateri** (144km ✝✕🖼) is one of my favourite villages. Pass above the Couvent de Marcasso on your right (where Walk 18 begins) and, on meeting the N197, turn left. Alternative walk 18 is based on **Lumio**★ (151km 🏔🏠△✕); you could enjoy an evening picnic at Occi, shown on page 88. The second turning left beyond Lumio leads to the 11th-century Romanesque San Pietro Church (✝), with its curious lion-headed portal. **Calvi** is straight on (161km).

# Bastia 1: SEASCAPES OF CAP CORSE

## Bastia • Macinaggio • Rogliano • Centuri-Port • Nonza • St-Florent • Patrimonio • Bastia

*Roads on the east coast are good; those on the west are narrow and often bumpy. All are winding. Be on the alert for livestock on the roadside along the west coast. Reckon on 137km/85mi, 5h driving. Note that although I think this is the most attractive way to do this tour, drivers with nervous passengers might prefer to do the whole circuit in reverse, so that the car is always on the inland side of the roads.*

En route: Walks 27, 28, 29, 33. Picnic suggestions for Walks 27 and 33 (both reached via bumpy tracks), but my favourite picnic spots on this tour are at Nonza (94.5km; see page 36).

C ap Corse stands apart from the rest of Corsica, both geographically and scenically. Contrasting coastal landscapes accompany you all the way on this tour: the east is gentle and subdued; the west sharp and dramatic. Watchtowers litter the countryside, and monasteries are as common as churches. Vestiges of the past lie around every corner. Small coves, some sandy, some pebbly, will draw you down to the magnetic turquoise sea. This excursion can be split into a leisurely two-day outing, the east coast one day, the west another.

Heading north on the D80 past **Pietranera** (3km ▲▲ ✕ ☻) and **Miomo** (5.5km 🏠 ▲▲ △ ✕), you're still in residential confines. Posh villas in choice locations overlook the sea. Pass the turn-off left for Pozzo, starting point for the ascent of **Monte Stello★**. At 1307m/4285ft, this is the second-highest summit on the cape (Walk 29). **Lavasina** (☨ ▲▲ ✕) is the site of one of the island's most important festivals (the Nativity of the Virgin, celebrated on the 8th September). The 17th-century church, Notre Dame des Graces (with an unsightly campanile) houses a painting of the Virgin and Child which is revered by fishermen and attributed with miraculous powers. Walk 28, a short (but still pretty stiff!) hike begins just by this church and climbs to the church at Pozzo, shown on page 108.

Before coming into **Erbalunga★** (10km 🏠 ▲▲ ☨ ✕), a favourite haunt of artists, you will spot it — a group of houses crammed onto a low spit of rock, sitting out in the water. The houses appear to 'grow' out of the sea. You can wander through the alleys of this curious old fishing village in five minutes. Four kilometres beyond Erbalunga, a balcony (☙) juts out of the hillside below the road. A tiny, rather special rocky cove sits out of sight to the right of it. It's an ideal swimming spot.

If you can chase up the key for the parish Church of St-Martin up in the Commune de Sisco (enquire in

advance at the Syndicat d'Initiative in Bastia), you may like to
look over its hoard of treasures:
the bit of soil from which God
made Adam, hairs from the
cloak of St John the Baptist, and
a fragment of a coat worn by the
Virgin Mary ... to mention but a
few. The turn-off for Sisco (D32) is
at **Marine de Sisco** (15.5km ▲△✕).
Once in **Sisco** (7km uphill), you'll have
another search for the key to the simple,
ideally-sited Romanesque San Michele Chapel (✝), not
far above St-Martin (✝). To get there, turn right past
St-Martin and take the first left, up a rough track. When
you come to another fork, park and walk up to the right.
Where the track swings left, continue along an overgrown
path. When you come to the remains of a stone building,
turn right along a hillside shelf and, 15 minutes from the
car, you're there. Don't worry if you forgot the key; you
have really climbed here for the views over the valley and
across the sea to the islands off Tuscany.

Return to the coastal road through this lush tree-rich
landscape, where hamlets of stone-built houses huddle
in the shade. Turn left and continue for another 2km, as
far as the turn-off for the Convent of Santa Catalina
(signposted 'Manoir Santa Catalina'). This monastery (✝)
is now an old people's home and occupies a fine perch
overlooking the sea. Beautifully restored, it has an
imposing fortified tower. Only the dilapidated church is
open to the public (key obtained in the home).

The countryside loses its trees; the turquoise-blue of
the sea deepens. **Marine de Pietracorbara** (20km
🔲▲✕), a pleasant resort of white sand set back in a U
in the coast, boasts the first substantial beach you reach.
The well-preserved Tour de l'Osse (🔲) serves as a
particularly striking landmark, further along the coast. A
pretty pebbly cove lies just below it. **Porticciolo** (26km
▲✕) is a small village overlooking the sea. A tiny marina
and narrow beach shelter in its shallow bay.

Beyond **Santa Severa** (28km ▲△✕🍽) the D80 continues past an unspoilt shingle beach, before reaching the
spread-out seaside village of **Marine de Meria** (34km
🔲▲). Some four kilometres further on lies the busy yacht-
ing harbour of **Macinaggio** (38.5km ▲△✕🍽). It sits at

33

*Santa Maria chapel and ruined tower (Walk 27, near Macinaggio)*

the end of a long sandy beach, which is excellent for the children. Access to Walk 27 begins on the road opposite the post office (small sign, 'Plage de Tamarone').

Continuing west, leave the D80 some 4km beyond Macinaggio: turn left (D53) for the historic **Commune de Rogliano** ★ (📷). This settlement of eight hamlets dominates the surrounding hills with its many prominent buildings, arousing your curiosity long before you reach it. In **Bettolacce** (44.5km 🏠♦️📷✕📷) you come face to face with the Eglise St-Agnel, set high on the hillside, from where there is a superb view down over Macinaggio and the setting for Walk 27. Below the church sits the Chapel of the Confrérie de Ste-Croix and below that, the impressive Tour Franceschi, standing guard over the hamlet. Passing through Bettolacce, return to the D80, remembering to look back at the scattering of mottled-grey houses ensconced amongst the trees. The ruins of the Convent of St Francis (♦️) are glimpsed on a hilltop above, and the view over Macinaggio's bay is superb.

Turn left on the D80, to look straight off the end of the cape to the sharp islet of la Giraglia. Winding around scrub-covered hills, you pass the Tollare/Barcaggio junction (possible 15.5km detour on a bumpy road to the curving sandy beach of Barcaggio (📷✕; visited on the long version of Walk 27). The main tour keeps to the D80, climbing to the **Col de la Serra** (📷). From here you can also walk (30min return) to the Moulin Mattei ★, an excellent viewpoint over the cape (take the first track off right).

Once over the pass, the more dramatic western coast unfolds before you (📷). Sheer hills rise straight up out of the sea. Villages nestle on protruding ridges. Turn off

34

*Centuri-Port, where you could have a lobster lunch instead of a picnic!*

*sharp right* on the D35 at **Camera** (50km), squeezing through the hamlet. Soon a medieval-style château is passed (∎), set amidst trees in a garden below the road. This 19th-century building belonged to General Cipriani. Head left at the fork beyond the château and wind down through olive trees and evergreen oaks. At a junction overlooking the scrub-covered Ilôt de Centuri, turn right for **Centuri-Port** ★ (54.5km ⛴ △✕). Parking in the village one-way system is sheer hell, but this port is definitely worth a stop. Lobsters are the speciality of the local fishermen, so if you feel like splurging, now is the time. The Sentier des Douaniers (see Walk 27) ends here.

From Centuri-Port, remain on the D35, keeping straight ahead for **Morsiglia** (59km). Some large rotund watch-towers dot the hills. Rejoining the D80, you head south around the seaside slopes. Shortly, a stunning bay, the Aliso Gulf, shines up at you. The grey collar of rock intensifies the contrast of forest-green vegetation and a crystalline blue sea. A steep rough track goes down to the beach, but it's best reached on foot. Notice the fascinating family mausoleums on this road, as you head towards Pino.*

---

*Should you wish to make a detour to the Genoese Tour de Sénèque ★ (photograph page 33), turn left just before Pino on the D180 signposted for Luri/Santa Severa. At the Col de Ste-Lucie (🚏), turn right up a side-road for 1km, and park in the grounds of a huge ruined building. This was once a famous boarding school — the most modern on Corsica, with central heating, library, and swimming pool. But when the villages around Luri built their own schools, the once-grand edifice fell into disrepair. The path to the tower starts here; it's steep and very slippery when wet; allow 1h20min return (a climb/descent of 120m/400ft).

**Pino** (69km 🛉🔺✕🚌📷) is a gracious hillside village, its houses scattered amidst a profusion of trees: cypress, palms, planes, oaks and olives. Looking back from here, you see sheer coastal ridges toppling off into the sea. The Convent of St Francis (🏠🛉), more impressive when seen from above, perches on a rocky shore down to the right. (The road to it is just 1km beyond Pino.) While the old convent now houses a private school, there is an interesting fresco in the chapel and a Genoese tower in the grounds.

The coastline becomes more exciting as you continue towards St-Florent. The D80 hangs out over sea cliffs that drop away into the indigo depths. Strips of overgrown terracing step stretches of near-vertical slopes; prickly-pear cactus is in its element. You pass through an outburst of jagged ridges and then curve inland up the Furcone Valley. Below is the Marine de Giottani, another pretty cove set in white rock. It quickly opens up into an irresistibly dazzling little beach. Most people drive past it slowly and, a minute later, turn round and go back to it. High above the sea again, an enormous building (which at first glance you might mistake for an hotel) disrupts the seascape. It's an abandoned asbestos mine. If you can ignore this awesome sight, you will enjoy the tremendous view across the hilly coastline towards the central massif and the bumpy Désert des Agriates. Black sand beaches lie below you here, further intensifying another colour contrast: white rock and royal-blue sea.

Your approach to **Nonza**★ (94.5km 🏠🛉🔺✕📷) is spectacular. Its captivating beach, a long wide band of pebbles made almost inaccessible by the sheer-sided hills that rise up out of it, spans out directly below you. The village is superbly sited, built into a rocky spur that leans out over the tail of the beach some 150m/500ft below. A tower, marking the site of a medieval fort, crowns the spur: this is an awe-inspiring perch and a delightful place to unpack the picnic basket. You have stupendous views down onto the beach and over the orange, lichen-covered slate roof-tops of the village, splashed with purple bougainvillaea. Nonza was the birthplace of Saint Julie, a martyr crucified by the Romans. A pilgrimage to the Fountain of St Julie and its altar is held each year on the 22nd of May. If you find the tower perch a little too precarious for lunch, this altar and the two gushing fountains make another lovely picnic spot: they are below the road, on the path to the beach (keep right at the fork).

Nonza's 16th-century church, with a tableau depicting St Julie, is above the road.

Closer to St-Florent, you begin descending. The coastline eases out and is less exciting visually. Some vineyards and orchards soothe your approach. Five kilometres before the town, at the Bastia junction, keep right on the D81. **St-Florent★** (114km ▮✝▲▲ ▲△✕➡⊕WC), where Walk 33 begins and ends, is an extremely pleasant resort. Set deep in the gulf, on the banks of the Alisio River, it clusters round a huge citadel that dominates the port. The Genoese part of the town (**Nebbio★**), however, sits 1km further inland. All that remains of it is the 12th-century cathedral church of Santa Maria Assunta, one of the island's masterpieces. (A sister edifice, La Canonica, may be visited during Tour 'Bastia 3'.) The key to this outstanding example of Romanesque architecture is obtainable (for a small deposit) from the *syndicat d'initiative* on the Bastia road.

Return along the D81 and turn right at the Bastia junction. Just inside **Patrimonio** (121km ✝▲▲ ✕), turn off left for the 16th-century Eglise St-Martin (✝). While the interior holds nothing of great interest, this elegant church, with its graceful steeple, is very photogenic. Before you reach it, notice the menhir (▮▮) in a garden on your left. Patrimonio is known for its private (as opposed to co-operative) vineyards; quality, not quantity, is the vintners' aim. You can sample reds, whites, rosés and muscatels.

The **Col de Teghime★** (🎦) is the pass that breaches the high hills separating St-Florent from Bastia. From here there is a grand panorama over the eastern and western side of the cape and, on hazeless days, towards Elba. Finer still are the views from the **Serra di Pigno★** (🎦): the signposted turn-off (D338) is on the left, just over the pass; the viewpoint is 4km uphill.

Return to the D81 and descend to **Bastia** (137km).

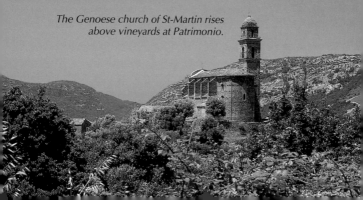

*The Genoese church of St-Martin rises above vineyards at Patrimonio.*

## Bastia 2: THE ROCK POOLS OF THE RESTONICA

### Bastia • Ponte Leccia • Corte • Gorges de la Restonica • (Murato • Défilé de Lancone) • Bastia

*The road to Corte is good, but the single-lane road in the Restonica Valley is very precipitous, and there are no barriers. Note that vehicles* ***descending*** *this road have right of way (in case of brake failure). Note also that there is a restriction on the size of vehicle that can use this road (some camper-vans are considered too wide), and that not all mopeds can handle the steep ascent. The detour route from Ponte Nuovo to Murato and the Défilé de Lancone is equally precipitous. These narrow roads may be closed in early spring and late autumn. Even if they are open, they are not recommended in bad weather: rock fall is common, and it can be very cold. Watch out for foraging animals. Reckon on 169km/105mi, 6h driving if you return via your outgoing route; add 34km/21mi, 1h30min if you return by the 'detour route'.*

En route: Walks 30, 31, 32; picnic suggestions for Walks 31 and 32. Walks 4-9, lovely excursions around Venaco and Vizzavona, each with a picnic suggestion, are easily reached from Corte.

Who needs beaches when there are rivers as beautiful as the Restonica? This breath-taking gorge merits a day out in everyone's holiday and, whatever you do, don't miss the lakes visited on Walk 31. Young belles struggle up to them in high heels, and babies go up on dad's back; everyone climbs to see the magnetic beauty of these mirror-like lakes. And when the day is ending, you can throw yourselves into one of the many delicious pools that fill the floor of the Restonica.

The tour follows the N193 from Bastia all the way to Corte. At **Casamozza** (20km ⛰▲✕⛽) you leave the coastal plains behind and come into the Golo Valley, a hilly unkempt area with small farm plots stretching across the narrow river flats. Danger signs warn against swimming in the river; they are there for a good reason! At **Ponte Nuovo** (38km ⛽) you pass the D5 to Murato, an optional detour for the homeward leg. The valley opens up: orchards, vineyards and hayfields cover the floor. Pass through **Ponte Leccia** (46km ⛰▲△✕⛽), the crossroads of the north, and follow the Golo River.

Crossing the San Quilico Pass, you leave the Golo Valley and descend to **Corte**★ (70km ♜✝⛰▲△✕⛽⊕📷**M**WC), Corsica's university town, set at the confluence of the Tavignano and Restonica rivers, in the shadow of the central massif. The surrounding countryside is pastoral and clear of maquis, with straw-coloured hills. Corte remains unaffected by tourism; plain, but pleasant tall buildings line the main street. The old quarter terraces a steep hillface, and a 15th-century fortress crowns the citadel. Corte is a fine base for walks and drives into the central mountains, around Venaco and Vizzavona.

*The 12th-century Pisan Romanesque church of San Michele di Murato rises in splendid isolation on a flat crest (detour route on the return to Bastia).*

The turn-off for Walk 30 is just before the Tavignano on the south side of town. Just *over* the river is the road to **La Restonica★**. Turn right on the D623 and head up alongside the bounding crystal-clear river (▲▲✕). Watch out for cows in the middle of the road! Climbing rapidly, you enter pines. Below the road, small inviting river flats, cushioned in grass and ferns and shaded by pines, make splendid picnic spots. Coming into alpine pastures, the pines subside and only a few grand species remain. Not far beyond the Pont de Grotelle (starting point for Walk 32), the road ends at the enchanting **Bergeries de Grotelle** (84.5km), a settlement of low stone houses and animal pens. If you're walking up to the lakes (*highly recommended;* see photographs pages 114 and 116), park here.

In hot weather you may want to end the excursion with a dip in one of those inviting pools further downstream, before returning the same way to **Bastia** (169km).

But if it's too cold or you would rather be driving, then take this long 'detour route' back. Just over the bridge at Ponte Nuovo, turn left on the D5 (signposted for Lento/ Bigorno). This ascent, along a very narrow road, affords views back down the Golo. Pass through Lento, a village set back on tree-patched slopes. As you enter Bigorno, the D5 swings up left to a pass, the Bocca di Bigorno★ (📷), from where there are fine views over the Golo to table-topped Monte San Petrone above the hills of la Castagniccia and Monte Sant' Angelu above Loreto. Over the pass, a rolling plateau stretches before you; then you descend through hills laced with chestnut groves. Beyond Murato (✕🍴), you soon spot the church of San Michele (✝) on a flat crest. From here you look down onto the Aliso basin, and the Gulf of St-Florent fills in the backdrop. Descending, you come to a roundabout: take the second exit (D62), into the Défilé de Lancone★. You'll get only a glimpse of the gorge on this hair-raising road where everyone toots with anxiety as they round each bend. But a superb view over the green-embroidered plains of Bastia and the Biguglia Lagoon greets you just before you leave the gorge. Turn left on the N193 to Bastia (203km).

39

# Bastia 3: LA CASTAGNICCIA'S CHESTNUT GROVES

**Bastia • Ponte Leccia • Morosaglia • la Porta • Piedicroce • Cervione • San Nicolao • Bastia**

*Some of the country roads followed on this tour are narrow and winding. Watch out for foraging livestock. There are no petrol stations between Ponte Leccia and Cervione (85km). Reckon on 172km/107mi, 5h30min driving.*

En route: Walk 34 (with picnic suggestion). There is another recommended picnic spot just before San Nicolao (127km).

*Bust of Pasquale Paoli in l'Ile-Rousse*

There are no real 'sights' on this tour; it is simply a most enjoyable day's outing in a landscape bumpy with hills and thick with the chestnut groves that give their name to the region, the Castagniccia. Small rustic villages echo the silence, with their shuttered houses and boarded-up churches. A pleasant surprise along the way: the old roadside fountains have been restored, given names, and gush forth water once again.

Follow Tour 'Bastia 2' to **Ponte Leccia** (46km). Just before crossing the Golo, turn left on the D71 for Morosaglia. Climbing amidst low abrupt hills, you overlook the Golo Valley. The Aig de Popolasca, a high craggy mass, rears up above the far valley wall. Further along to the left the great Rotondo massif is seen. Junipers and pines share the lower slopes; higher up, cork trees stand out with their crusty bark. (You'll often see a large square piece neatly cut out of the trunk. These trees can only be stripped when 25 years old — and then only once every 10-12 years.)

Travelling east, you skirt the upper Golo Valley and look out over the hills above Ponte Nuovo (the 'detour route' in Car tour 'Bastia 2'). **Morosaglia** (60.5km ♣M) has a claim to fame: Pasquale Paoli, Corsica's great patriot, was born here. His birthplace is a museum (open daily 09.00-12.00; 15.00-18.00). The Romanesque church of Santa Reparata, where he was baptised, sits above the village; his school (the present village school and named for him) is the grand building on the right as you enter the village. It was formerly the Rostino Monastery and a meeting place for members of the Corsican Liberation Movement in the early 18th century. This pretty village lies scattered deep in the hills amidst chestnut groves. The name of the region, **la Castagniccia ★**, derives from the Latin word for sweet chestnut — once the mainstay of the

40

local people. Not only was the flour an important part of their diet and the wood used for furniture, farm tools and fuel, but both were bartered for goods from other regions.

Beyond Morosaglia, you come to the Col de Prato (☞ ▲※M), where you can park for Walk 34. Just over the pass, there is a fascinating museum of Corsican artefacts in the pleasant hotel/restaurant (they will light it up on request). Now the sea reappears in the distance over the hills. The rugged inland Fium' Altu, a valley of ridges and hills saturated in trees, stretches out before you. Hamlets lie sporadically dispersed across the inclines. Not far below the pass (some 5km from Morosaglia), turn *sharp left* on a narrow road that swings downhill towards la Porta (signposted). This lovely road (D205) twirls its way round the hillsides under an arcade of trees. The countryside is crisp with arboreal greenery. You squeeze through and then past a couple of old grey hamlets. Just after you join a road coming from the left, **la Porta ★** (72km ♣▲※) comes into sight, adorning the crest of a declining ridge. The church campanile immediately steals your attention. This elegant, oriental-looking bell tower is supposedly the finest baroque tower on the island but, once alongside it, you discover that the 1720 structure has suffered a rather heavy-handed facelift. Park in the square and visit the church however: it's so seldom that one finds a church open on this island! The interior of St-Jean-Baptiste is lavishly decorated, with a beautifully-painted organ loft. Time for morning coffee? Find the *boulangérie*, buy some custard tarts and head over to the café. Then continue on through **Croce** (78km **M** of local customs, open Sat/Sun afternoons only). **Monte San Petrone ★** (1767m/5795ft; photograph page 122), the goal of Walk 34, is the most prominent upthrust in the area, with its rocky crest.

Return to the D71 and turn left. This is the route of the drinking fountains: many are lovingly restored, and all are different. Art enthusiasts may like to summon up the energy to locate the key for the Church of St André in **Campana** (83km ♣) and then climb up to it. It holds a painting attributed to Zubarán or one of his pupils. Here Monte San Petrone rises up just beside you.

The Orezza Monastery (♣) is the impressive skeleton of a building you pass further on, draped in creepers. Once a seat for the Corsican Liberation Movement, this is where Paoli was elected Commander-in-Chief of the Corsican National Guard. It was destroyed in 1943. Further along you enter **Piedicroce** (87km ♣▲※) and

pass the massive church of St Peter and St Paul, with a
17th-century organ said to be the oldest on Corsica and
a 16th-century painting on wood of the Virgin and Child.
Entering **Carcheto-Brustico★** (90.5km 🛉), a narrow lane
off left descends to the church of St Margaret, where (if
you can find the key) you would see two works of local
origin, an alabaster statuette and a painting of the Stations
of the Cross in a Corsican setting.

The **Bocca d'Arcarota** (✕🖭) opens your way to the
vast Alesani Valley, flooded with trees. The sinuous road
describes a deep V, where the cloak of deciduous trees
fades out, and a tangle of maquis takes over. The twisting
tail of the Alesani Dam soon catches your eye in the valley
floor, with its cloudy-green water. An unmarked lay-by
(🖭) affords a good view over the dam.

Continuing the descent, your view stretches all along
the undulating sea plain. **Cervione** (121km 🛉▲✕🛏M
🖭) is a balcony village, hooded by chestnuts and olive
trees. The imposing church here, St Mary and St Erasmus,
dwarfs even the tall houses that surround it. The Bishop's
Palace (noticeably renovated) houses a museum of local
archaeology (open daily except Sun/hol: 10.00-12.00;
14.30-18.00). Just beyond Cervione, visit the chapel of
Santa Cristina★ (🛉). Ask for the key at the *mairie*/school
in **Valle-di-Campoloro**, 0.5km outside Cervione. Then
turn left off the D71, down a country lane, just beyond
the *mairie*. Fork left again 1km down, onto a dirt track
signposted 'Santa Maria'. (Better still, walk; the track is
very bumpy.) The chapel holds exquisite 15th-century
frescoes: the pastel colours are still sharp, the facial
expressions still very clearly defined.

From here return to the San Nicolao junction (D330)
and turn right. Beyond a tunnel you look straight up into
a couple of small waterfalls that leap down from a gap in
the hillside. A path climbing above the lay-by takes you
to them. At this ideal picnic spot, you'll find a shallow
pool. Coming into **San Nicolao** (127km 🛉▲ ✕), a shady
hillside village, you come to an intersection (🖭) with a
fine view over a solitary 17th-century baroque church
with a six-storied campanile (🛉). Head right on the D34
and, at the N198 turn left, back to **Bastia** (172km).*

---

*A detour may be made on the homeward route: take the airport exit,
then turn right immediately on the D107, to visit La Canonica (🛉), one
of Corsica's finest churches (Romanesque, 12c). The ancient city of
Mariana was founded here in 93BC. The 11th-century church of San
Parteo (🛉) is nearby. Continue to Bastia via the pretty lagoon.

## Porto-Vecchio: THE OSPEDALE AND BAVELLA MASSIFS, AND A SUNSET OVER BONIFACIO

**Porto-Vecchio • l'Ospédale • Zonza • Col de Bavella • Solenzara • Pinarellu • San Cipriano • Plage de Palombaggia • Bonifacio • Porto-Vecchio**

*The roads are good but very winding. However, a 30km-long stretch between Argiavara and Solenzara is very narrow and potholed. In bad weather the first part of the tour (as far as Solenzara) is not recommended, due to poor visibility and the possibility of rockfall. Always be alert for foraging livestock. The high passes can be very cold, with gale-force winds. Reckon on 217km/135mi; about 7h driving.*

En route: Walks 35, 36, 37, 38, 39, 40 (all with picnic suggestions)

Ideally this drive should be a leisurely two-day affair, so that you can fit in several short, very spectacular walks, through some of the island's most impressive pink-granite mountains. But if you can't wait until tomorrow, make a mad dash to Bonifacio, to watch the sun set over the island's most dramatic town.

Setting out on the D368 from Porto-Vecchio, head towards Zonza, through countryside lightly wooded in the cork trees for which this region is well known. Their stripped trunks are a curious sight. A winding road leads you into the large sprawling hills on the spine of the Ospédale massif, which is home to a splendid forest of maritime pines. You enjoy stunning views over the deeply-etched Golfe de Porto-Vecchio and inland along the wide, open Stabiacco Valley that stretches back off the gulf. Bright green fields lining the valley floor stand out in this otherwise dark green countryside.

**L'Ospédale** (19km ✕ 📷) takes its name from the hospital that was on this site in Roman times. It commands a magnificent panorama over the gulfs of Porto-Vecchio and Santa Manza. A small summer retreat, its granite-block houses sit well camouflaged high on the wooded hillside amidst great boulders of granite. Your first chance for a walk comes up just 1km outside l'Ospédale, where a road leads left to 'Agnarone'. This may be too far off your route during this long car tour (see map at the bottom of page 130), but Walk 39 *is a must* at some point during your time in the south, especially if you visit in spring.

Continuing on the D368, you wind through the forest. Huge mounds of rock grow out of the cover of trees. You skirt the **Barrage de l'Ospédale★** (📷), a glimmering reservoir that lies at the foot of Punta di Corbu. After crossing the dam wall, watch for the 'La Cascada' snack bar, on your right, 1km along. This is the starting point for Walk 37 to the **Cascade de Piscia di Gallo★**, illustrated on page 128). A third chance to stretch your legs comes up at the **Bocca d'Illarata** (991m/3250ft), where the ascent of Monte Calva begins (Walk 38). But it's the many facets of the Punta di u Diamanti just off the road that catch the eye (photograph page 129).

Over the pass you descend through forest (△) into **Zonza** (40.5km 🏔🗙🚻). Chestnut trees announce the beginning of this village. It sits at crossroads, deep in the hills. Here turn right on the D268 and climb to the **Col de Bavella★** (1218m/4000ft; 49km 📷) — one of Corsica's most breath-taking viewpoints. The impenetrable valley walls, with their needle-sharp crags (the 'Aiguilles de Bavella') can be anything from a deep red to a soft rose

*The Barrage de l'Ospédale, at the foot of Punta di Corbu*

colour. Seeing is believing! Large windswept pines stand here on the pass, as does a statue to Our Lady of the Snows. The hamlet of **Bavella** (♠✗) huddles just over the pass. A small gathering of stone, wood and corrugated iron dwellings, it is more like a pastoral outpost than a hamlet. Walks 35 and 36 begin opposite the inn (photographs pages 124 and 126).

You descend in hairpin bends through a valley dominated by towering granite walls. Notice the flat-topped pines: this is not the latest fashion in tree trimming; the strong winds are to blame. On the lower inclines you wend your way through plantations of firs, young pines, and chestnut trees. Closer to the valley floor, keep an eye open for a rocky outcrop that resembles a sitting dog (a terrier?). It's on a ridge on your left, about 15km downhill.

Once on the valley floor, you're in the company of the Solenzara River, a wide bouldery river bordered by beach-like stretches of sand. River swimmers will want to take a dip in its inviting pools, which are suitable for children. When you meet the N198, turn right to pass through the sea-side town of **Solenzara** (80km ♠△✗ ♠⊕) and follow the coast back to Porto-Vecchio. This stretch of coastline is flat and rocky, with a few pleasant beaches collaring the small bays. You pass behind the sweeping beaches of **Favone** (92km ♠♠△✗) and **Tarco** (96km ♠♠△✗). Curving round into an open bay, you spot a Genoese tower on a promontory, the Punta di Fautea (100km ⊡△✗).

Turning inland, the N198 soon enters **Ste-Lucie-de-Porto-Vecchio** (105km ♠♠✗♠). Branch off left here onto the D168a, to see some of Porto-Vecchio's best-known beaches. Outside high season, **Pinarellu** (108km ⊡♠♠ △✗♠) is a quiet unassuming resort, sitting in a deep bay and guarded by a Genoese tower set on a tiny islet. It boasts a fine beach bordered with pines. A pretty rural drive over a sometimes narrow and bumpy road leads you along the D468 to the next resort: some 8km from Pinarellu turn off left on the D668. After 1km you come to a sweeping sandy beach at **San Ciprianu** (118km ♠♠△✗♠). If these first two beaches didn't take your fancy however, then try the next turn off to the left, the D468a, to the fine beach at **Cala Rossa** (♠♠♠△✗).

Continuing along the D468, you pass behind ritzy **Golfo di Sogno** (♠♠✗), which also offers good swimming in its sheltered bay. Further on, you're distracted by the prominent chain of inland mountains and the bay, with the fortified town of Porto-Vecchio on the far side. Decide now whether to call it a day or make for Bonifacio.

At the roundabout you encounter just outside Porto-Vecchio (128km) keep right for Bonifacio, to bypass the centre. Just beyond the sixth roundabout, turn left on the Palombaggia road, to see the island's most highly-rated beach. Circling the Stabiacco estuary, you look across the reedy tidal river with its pine-studded sand banks, to Porto-Vecchio (🚗). A small pass takes you over the hills to **Piccovagia**. From here you may wish to make a detour to the Pointe de la Chiappa (🚗▲; add 6km return). If so, take the first left turn, following signs for 'Village de Vacance la Chiappa'. Immediately into the turn-off, go left again on a bumpy dirt track to the lighthouses. From the top of the crest between the two lighthouses (military and civilian) you have an impressive view over the bays of San Cipriano and Stagnolo, and onto the mountainous backdrop. On the left side of the point lie some rocky islets, the Iles Cerbicale.

The main tour continues straight through Piccovagia; after 1.5km, fork left for the **Plage de Palombaggia**★ (150km 🏖▲△✕). This long unspoilt beach with its crystal-clear water, red rock, and low sand dunes is shaded by beautiful umbrella-shaped parasol pines. It would be easy just to lose the rest of the day here.

Return to the junction for the beach and turn left. More of this vast beach reveals itself through the trees along the shore. Sadly, the buildings do little to help conserve this very special stretch of coastline. At the village of **Bocca dell' Oro** (160km ✕) keep right to rejoin the N198, where you turn left for Bonifacio. Heading through low hills wooded in cork trees and maquis, you eventually join the N196 and come into **Bonifacio**★ (187km ✝🏖▲△✕🚗 WC 🚗). The most convenient car park is on the left on entering the harbour complex. To visit the citadel and old town, follow Avenue Charles de Gaulle (at the right of the hospital), to climb above the port. This magnificently-sited town overhangs the sea from its cliff-top perch (cover photograph). Set on a high, narrow headland, Bonifacio enjoys superb sea views on both sides. To the south it looks along the dramatic, glaring-white sea cliffs, to the north down into the fjord-like inlet, and inland to the Cagna hills. Walk around the old town, inside the imposing and solid citadel walls. The elegant old buildings that line the narrow and shady streets are treasures of history. Visit the Eglise Sainte-Marie-Majeure, built by

*Seascapes on Walk 40 from Bonifacio (see also photograph page 133)*

both the Pisans (in the late 12th century) and the Genoese. Its tall campanile dates back to the 14th and 15th centuries. The relics of St Boniface, the town's patron saint, are kept here, together with a piece of the 'True Cross'. Other churches of interest are St-François (1390) and St-Dominique, a Gothic church started in 1270 by the Knights Templar and finished by the Dominicans in 1343. The pillars of this latter church (between the aisles and the nave) have small paintings dating from the 18th century, representing the Fifteen Mysteries of the Rosary.

If you're spending the day at Bonifacio, among the more popular beaches are Calalonga, Rondinara, and those in the Golfe de Santa-Manza. Or you may want to take one of the boat trips on offer ... perhaps to the small granite Iles de Lavezzi, which boast a variety of unusual flora. Another popular excursion is to the sea caves, where you can see the famous 'King of Aragon's Staircase' with its 187 steps. Sardinia is also easily accessible from here. If you want to keep driving, visit the **Ermitage de la Trinité ★** (✝), 7km west of Bonifacio: head west towards Sartène and take the first left turn off the N196. This ancient sanctuary is the sight of a local pilgrimage, but it's best known for its striking view back onto Bonifacio. Finally, don't miss Walk 40. Of course you *can* explore **Capo Pertusato ★** by car, but the road is closed beyond the semaphore; the lighthouse at the end of the cape is only accessible on foot. And you miss most of the dramatic coastline if you drive. Sunset is a fine time to end Walk 40, when the cliffs are aglow.

From Bonifacio take the N198 straight back to **Porto-Vecchio** (217km).

# 🌸 Walking

This book describes more than 50 different walking routes, chosen for their accessibility from the centres most popular with holidaymakers and covering a good cross-section of the island's varied landscapes. Since there are books already available on mountain climbing and the GR20 (including the well-known 'Topo Guides'), and since it will be quite hot when most 'Landscapers' visit Corsica, I have emphasised the less strenuous routes — walks that can be completed in a day's outing from your overnight base. *There are walks for all ages and abilities.*

The Parc Régional de la Corse has established six excellent long-distance trails. Of these, the best known is the GR20. More recent and less strenuous routes are two 'Mare e Monti' ('Sea and Mountains') footpaths, one in the north and another in the south, and three 'Mare a Mare' ('Sea to Sea') paths — in the north, centre and south. All are well-waymarked and dotted with refuges.

Corsica is a walkers' paradise. The grants the island has received from the EU have been mostly spent on protecting the environment and developing new walks (in contrast to most other areas of southern Europe!) There are various local walks ('Sentiers de Pays'), based on centres like Venaco. Private land abutting the sea has been purchased to create miles of coastal paths, and the Office National des Forêts has developed nature trails in the woodlands. Many of these trails, as well as easier stretches of the GR20, form part of the walks in this book. For more information about local walks in your area, contact the nearest tourist office *(syndicat d'initiative).*

## Maps and guides
The **maps** in this book (scale 1:50,000) should be sufficient for all the walks described. They are based on the latest IGN 'Top 25' (1:25,000) maps; the number of the relevant sheet is shown at the beginning of each walk, under 'Equipment'. Should you wish to go further afield, these maps are available everywhere on Corsica. The headquarters of the Parc Régional de la Corse (2, rue Major Lambroschini, Ajaccio; tel: 04 95 51 79 10) will be happy to provide up-to-date leaflets or give you the names of **guides** covering the area you wish to explore.

# Where to stay

The walks have been written up from four bases: **Ajaccio/Porto, Calvi, Bastia** and **Porto-Vecchio**. Not only are these the most popular tourist areas, but they are also quite well served by public transport.

The independent traveller will find **hotels, apartments, *pensions*** and **camp sites** in most corners of the island. However, many are only open from June 15th to September 15th. *Note:* In July and August nearly all the accommodation is booked — some of it months in advance. During June and September, reserving a couple of days in advance is usually sufficient, but not in the peak months! The rates for accommodation outside July and August are also far more reasonable than in high season. Never be afraid to ask for a discount out of season.

***Gîtes*** (country cottages) are also widely scattered across the island. These are usually rented by the week or month. ***Gîtes d'étape*** are inns geared for long-distance walkers and cyclists, with shared rooms. Meals are usually provided — and the cooking is often superb. For information (in English) see www.gites-corsica.com.

***Refuges*** are liberally dotted around the central mountains. Part of the GR20/Mare e Monti/Mare a Mare programme, they are well maintained, open all year round, and fully equipped (gas, kitchen utensils, beds, etc).

# Weather

**Mid-June until mid-September** is most reliable for walking on Corsica — and for swimming, too. On either side of this 'high season', the weather can be changeable, which means that some of the mountain walks can be extremely dangerous. Snow may lie as low as 1000m/ 3300ft in June and may fall again late in September.

In **May** and **October** you will usually encounter more good days than bad ones, but be sure of the weather before setting off for the mountains. Cloud or mist sometimes descends without warning, and the temperatures fall rapidly. May and October are best suited for walks below 1000m. The weather, even if it turns bad, is not usually bad enough to ruin an entire day, but it can get very cold. These are, however, the months of the flowers and autumnal colours. In spring the countryside is scented with the strong perfume of the maquis; in autumn the beech and chestnut groves are an extravaganza of yellows and golds, and the shepherds return with their flocks — a wonderful sight.

**July** and **August** are the really hot months, with temperatures in the 30s. Things to fear are dehydration, frightening electrical storms and forest fires. *Always carry plenty of water;* many mountain streams dry up in the summer. **Electrical storms** usually come with plenty of warning: *quickly* seek shelter away from exposed places.

As a general rule, the north of Corsica is hotter than the south, and the east is wetter than the west. And Ajaccio boasts the most sunshine in the whole of France.

**Wind patterns** on the island make for quite a study! Here are some names you might hear or see in the papers:

*Libeccio:* a strong wind from the southwest, hot and dry in summer; in winter it carries rain to the west;

*Maestral:* the Corsican version of the *mistral,* this wind comes from the northwest and is unpleasant all year round, with a whining violence. Fortunately, it blows infrequently;

*Sirocco:* a dry dusty wind from the southeast;

*Grecale:* blowing from the northeast, it carries rain to the north, but leaves the south unaffected;

*Tramontane:* a dry cold wind from the north, it blows very infrequently, but is strong enough to knock you off your feet;

*Mezzogiorno:* the 'midday' wind, caused by the interaction of the hot sun and the still-cold sea; it raises strong sea breezes along the coast.

Most bars and cafés have the local newspaper *(Corse Matin)* available, with **diagrammatic weather maps**.

# What to take

If you've come to Corsica without any special equipment such as a rucksack or walking boots, you can still do many of the walks — or you can buy the basic equipment on the island. *Don't* attempt the more difficult walks without the proper gear. For each walk in the book, the *minimum* year-round equipment is listed. Above all, you need stout, thick-soled shoes or walking boots. *Ankle support* is always advisable and is *essential* on some of the walks, where the path descends steeply over loose stones. You may find the following checklist useful:

stout shoes with ankle support or walking boots
waterproof rain gear (outside summer)
long trousers, tight at the ankles
sunhat, sunglasses, suncream
anorak (zip opening)
small rucksack
knives and openers
lightweight fleece

extra pair of long socks
telescopic walking stick(s)
whistle, torch, compass
plastic groundsheet
up-to-date timetable
spare bootlaces
gloves
tissues
insect repellent
antiseptic cream

jacket or woollen shirt
bathing wear
water bottle, plastic plates, etc
long-sleeved shirt (sun protection)
first aid kit, including bandages and plasters
'Dog Dazer' (see 'Things that bite ...', page 51)

At the top of each walk I recommend only the *special* equipment you might need; use the list opposite as a reminder, and go equipped according to the terrain and the season. *Always carry ample sun protection and plenty of water, and* **always be fully equipped for all extremes of weather**. Every year deaths are reported, and these are almost invariably caused through lack of caution.

# Language

English is not usually understood outside the principal tourist areas, but everyone speaks French. The local language *(lingua corsa)* is widely spoken (and now taught in all schools and colleges). If you speak Italian you will be understood, and to a certain degree understand the island dialect, since it is similar to peninsular Tuscan. Try to learn at least a few words of greeting and thanks in the local language — your efforts will be greatly appreciated.

Corsican spellings are widely used for place names, but these may vary even when referring to the same place! You will spot inconsistencies in the text, on maps, and on local signposts; unfortunately, this is unavoidable.

# Things that bite, sting, or shoot

**Dogs** are not generally a problem on Corsica, since most of the time you'll be far from habitation. In summer, however, some of the shepherds' dogs may send shivers down your spine. Let the shepherd know you're around, and you won't have any worries. Lone country houses always have a guard dog … or three. Watch their tails and heed their barks and growls. If you're worried, you could invest in an ultrasonic 'Dog Dazer': these can be bought on the Sunflower web site (www.sunflowerbooks.co.uk).

The **shooting season** for all game is from the third Sunday in August until the first Sunday in January. Some bird-shooting extends until the end of March. It can be very unnerving to have hunters blasting away all around you! If you fear they are too close, don't be afraid to bellow out — in *any* language!

You'll be pleased to read that while **snakes** and **insects** are to be found on the island, none has a fatal bite or sting.

# Waymarking

**Waymarking** is consistent on the GR20 (red/white flashes) and the 'Mare e Monti' and 'Mare a Mare' trails (orange flashes). But local walks use various colours (which change from year to year), signposts … or nothing at all. Nature trails are often marked with wooden posts.

# A country code for walkers and motorists

The experienced rambler is used to following a 'country code', but the tourist out for a lark may unwittingly cause damage, harm animals, and even endanger his own life. Do heed this advice:

- **Do not light fires.** Stub out cigarettes with care.
- **Do not frighten animals.** The livestock you will encounter when touring and walking are not tame. By making loud noises or trying to touch or photograph them, you may cause them to run in fear and be hurt.
- **Walk quietly** through all farms, hamlets and villages, **leaving all gates just as you found them.**
- **Protect all wild and cultivated plants.** Don't try to pick wild flowers or uproot saplings. Obviously fruit and crops are someone's private property and should not be touched. *Never walk over cultivated land.*
- **Take all your litter away with you.**

The following points cannot be stressed too strongly:

— **Do not take risks.** Do not attempt walks beyond your capacity and **never walk alone**. Four people make the best walking group: in case of injury, someone can stay with the injured person, while two go for help. Always tell a responsible person *exactly* where you are going and what time you plan to return: if your party is lost or one of your group is injured, rescue services would be notified that much more quickly.

— **At any time a walk may become unsafe** due to fire or storm damage, or the havoc caused by bulldozers. If the route is not as described in this book, and your way ahead is not secure, do *not* attempt to continue.

— **Strenuous walks** are unsuitable in high summer.

— **Mountain walks** are unsuitable in wet weather.

— **Do not overestimate your energy**: your speed will be determined by the slowest walker in the group.

— **Transport** at the end of the walk may be vital.

— **Proper shoes or boots** are a necessity.

— **Warm clothing** is needed in the mountains; even in summer, take something appropriate with you, in case you are delayed or injured.

— **Extra food and drink** should be taken on long walks.

— **Always take a sunhat**; cover arms and legs as well on sunny days.

# Organisation of the walks

The 40 main walks in this book are grouped in four sections, chiefly for the ease of those travelling by public transport (or hiring a taxi): Ajaccio/Porto (Walks 1-15), Calvi (Walks 16-26), Bastia (Walks 27-34) and Porto-Vecchio (Walks 35-40). If you have a car, naturally a far greater range of rambles will be within easy reach.

I hope that the book is set out so that you can plan you walks easily — depending on how far you want to g your abilities and equipment … and what time you are willing to get up in the morning! You might begin by considering the fold-out touring map inside the back cover. Here you can see at a glance the overall terrain, the road and rail network, and the location of all the walks.

Quickly flipping through the book, you'll find that there is at least one photograph for every walk. Having selected one or two potential excursions from the map and the photographs, look over the planning information at the beginning of the walks. Here you'll find distance/ walking time, grade, equipment, how to get there by public transport, and where to park if you are travelling by car. If the walk appears to be beyond your fitness or ability, check to see if a short or alternative version is described, which *would* appeal to you. On very hot days, the Short walks and Picnic suggestions may be as strenuous an adventure as you'd like to tackle.

When you are on your walk, you will find that the text begins with an introduction to the overall landscape and then quickly turns to a detailed description of the route itself. The large-scale walking maps (all scale 1:50,000) have been specially annotated to show key landmarks and, where possible, set out facing the walking notes. Times are given for reaching certain points in the walk. I have tried to estimate these times for the average, reasonably-fit walker. So if you're a beginner, or if you prefer a leisurely pace, a walk may take you **much longer**. Don't forget to take transport connections at the end of the walk into account! The most important factor is *consistency* of walking times, and I suggest that you compare your times with mine on one or two short walks, before you embark on a long hike.

Below is a **key to the symbols** used on the maps:

| | | | |
|---|---|---|---|
| ▬▬▬ | primary road | 🚗 🚌 | car parking.bus stop |
| ═══ | secondary road | 🚌 | railway station |
| ═══ | minor road | ⚹ | spring, fountain, waterfall |
| ──── | motorable or other track | ● | water tank, reservoir |
| ─ ─ ─ ─ | cart track | *P* | recommended picnic spot |
| ········ | footpath | ▱ ☰ | best views.picnic tables |
| ▬2→ | walking route and direction | ■ △ | building.campsite |
| ▬2→ | alternative route | ⚑ ⚔ | transmitter.quarry |
| ─150─ | height (m) | 🚁 | helicopter landing pad |
| ☗ † ⊡ | church.cross.cemetery | ─··─··─ | railway.railway tunnel |
| ■ ⋔ | castle or fort.ancient site | ⊟ | sports ground |
| ✹ ✕ ⊡ | mill.windmill.watchtower | ❗ | danger of vertigo! |

# 1  POINTE DE LA PARATA • ANSE DE MINACCIA • POINTE DE LA PARATA

**Distance/time:** 13.5km/8.4mi; 2h50min

**Grade:** easy, but some thorny scrub on route. No shade on beaches, can be very hot. Overall ascents/descents of 150m/490ft.

**Equipment:** as page 50; light shoes, sun protection, bathing things and plenty of water recommended; *IGN map 4153 OT*

**Access:** 🚗 or 🚌 (Timetable 1) to/from the Pointe de la Parata

**Alternative walk: Pointe de la Parata — Capigliolo — D111** (12km/ 7.4mi; 2h45min; grade as main walk, but with overall ascents and descents of 250m/820ft). Access by bus as above. Follow the main walk to the Anse de Minaccia. Then return to Capigliolo, climb the motorable track up to the D111b, and turn right downhill to the D111 (bus stop).

**Short walks/picnic suggestions**

**1**  **Tour de la Parata** (1.5km/1mi; 20min; easy). Stroll around the tower, or climb up to it. This setting is best enjoyed under a setting sun, when the Iles Sanguinaires give off a pinkish glow, and all the day trippers have gone home.

**2**  **Pointe de la Corba** (2.8km/1.7mi; 1h05min; easy). Follow the main walk to the rocky cove just beyond the Pointe de la Corba (30min) and return the same way.

This walk is an excellent 'starter' and puts you into the holiday mood straight away. It's easy, gives you a taste of the beaches to come, and takes you through picturesque countryside. In spring you'll be intoxicated by the sweet-smelling maquis, when the hillsides are ablaze with a riot of brightly-coloured flowers.

**The walk begins** at the **Pointe de la Parata**. This rocky promontory is the site of a 17th-century Genoese tower, built as a defence against the Moors. Beyond the point lie the Iles Sanguinaires, a group of sharp granite islets. Take the gravelly path at the left-hand side of the restaurant; you're immediately swallowed up in maquis, a low mat of Mediterranean scrub.* An array of spring flowers holds your attention all along, and yellow spiny broom lights up the hillsides. You head round into a aquamarine-coloured bay, set at the foot of dark green hills. Vivid carmine *Lampranthus* covers the banks.

Rising to a large rectangular RUIN WITH TWO DOORWAYS (an old rifle range; **10min**), you will see your ongoing route ahead: a dirt track following the west coast. Make your way over to it, maybe in the company of the odd car bumping along to one of the flower-filled weekend retreats. Notice the pink-and-yellow-coloured rock on

*In early summer this path — one of the loveliest stretches on the walk — may be overgrown with head-high lacerating maquis. If it is impassable when you visit, walk (or drive) 700m back along the D111: 200m before the tennis courts (parking), walk uphill to a large rectangular ruin with two doorways and join the walk at the 10min-point.

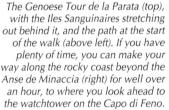

*The Genoese Tour de la Parata (top), with the Iles Sanguinaires stretching out behind it, and the path at the start of the walk (above left). If you have plenty of time, you can make your way along the rocky coast beyond the Anse de Minaccia (right) for well over an hour, to where you look ahead to the watchtower on the Capo di Feno.*

the hillock over to the left. After crossing a low crest above the **Pointe de la Corba** (**30min**), you look down into a small rocky cove. The track descends to it (a good place to end Short walk 2 with a picnic), but you bear right, along the wide path. Lizards galore dart across your path, as you brush your way through flowers.

As you cross over a ridge (**1h**), a superb view greets you: two beautiful beaches rest in the now-flat coastline: the first is small and circular, the second large and sweeping. The white sand glares in the sunlight. An open grassy valley, sheltered by high rocky hills, empties out into the bay. The arm of the cape rolls gently out to the left. Descending, you soon come to a track above the first

cove, to find the little holiday hamlet of **Capigliolo**. Make your way down the steps by the wall and onto the beach, the **Plage de St-Antoine (1h12min)**.

At the end of this blinding-white cove, squeeze through the rocks and mount the bank to continue along the shore. Just beyond the next cove, a clearer path leads you to the **Anse de Minaccia (1h25min)**. The countryside here is completely unspoiled. Cows graze in the fields, and nudists loaf on the beach. I'll bet I know which gets your attention first!

It's possible to continue along the coast for another hour or more, to take in more inviting, usually-deserted coves. But the main walk ends here: return the same way to the **Pointe de la Parata (2h50min)**, or take the inland route via the track from Capigliolo (Alternative walk).

## 2 ROCHER DES GOZZI

See map opposite, below     **Distance/time:** 7.5km/4.7mi; 3h30min

**Grade:** moderate-strenuous, with an ascent/descent of 340m/1115ft. The (somewhat overgrown) paths are slippery when wet. You must be sure-footed and have a head for heights to reach the rock itself.

**Equipment:** as page 50; walking boots, sun protection, long trousers and ample water recommended; *IGN map 4153 OT*

**Access:** 🚗 to/from the cemetery in Appietto (north of the Col de Listin-cone on the D81). Or 🚌 to/from the Col de Listincone (Timetables 2, 3) and walk the 2.5km/1.5mi to Appietto (add 200m/650ft of ascent; 25min); return to the col for your bus.

The Rocher des Gozzi is the most noticeable landmark in the Gravona Valley northeast of Ajaccio. Every time you leave the town, there it stands — a solid mass of bare rock rising straight up off the plains. The best time to end this walk is in the evening, when the soft rose colour of the rock intensifies under the fading light. The stupendous panorama from the summit is ample reward for the climb the walk entails.

**Start out** some 40m/yds south of the CEMETERY in **Appietto**. Turn right on a dirt track and follow it over to the **Chapelle San Chirgu** on the ridge opposite. From here you have a fine view of Appietto, a village dating from the Middle Ages, once the home of the Counts of Cinarca. It consists of three separate hamlets: the highest, with its miniature castle, and the lowest, with its lovely mansions, are the more picturesque.

Your continuing route lies along the ridge directly to the east, but the old path has been fenced off. Walk *back* from the chapel for about 100m/yds (just where the track bends left), then take the narrower track heading uphill to the right. When it ends at a gate, head right, through the fencing, and climb steeply uphill. (This path will be quite overgrown, until it becomes established as the main path up to the ridge.) When you meet the main path on the ridge, follow it to the left uphill (but first leave a marker, to find this descent point on your return).

As you ascend, the hills fold back, and the vast Golfe d'Ajaccio comes into view. On your right you look down onto the Lava Valley, ensconced in the hills running up from the Lava Gulf. The Punta Pozzo di Borgo is the highest of these hills, and the isolated Château de la Punta stands out, perched on its slopes. It belongs to the Pozzo di Borgo family, descendants of Charles André Pozzo di Borgo, Napoleon's great enemy.

Brushing through the dense flora (watch for tiny pink butterfly orchids), your way splinters and rejoins: remain

57

*Rocher des Gozzi from just below the Col de Listincone*

on the crest. If you find yourself fenced in (**1h**), scramble up to a large rock which enables you to step over the fence. Several minutes later, pass through a collapsed stone wall that runs straight down the spine of the ridge. Now you're on its right-hand flanks, and a rock 'balcony' serves as as excellent viewing point minutes later.

*Watch carefully* for the point where your path forks off right (**1h15min**) around the hillside towards the Rocher des Gozzi. No obvious landmarks are here to alert you, but at this point you are in a small clearing and just below a hilltop. The rock itself looks about at eye level. Follow this goats' trail (a short stretch of path a minute along might prove unnerving for inexperienced walkers). You round a fold in the slope and look straight across to the impressive rock … and Ajaccio. The way divides once in a while, so just contour, following either path. The hillside drops off into a precipitous wall down to the plain.

In half an hour you're on a saddle alongside the STONE RUIN (**1h45min**) glimpsed from your earlier viewpoint. The **Rocher des Gozzi** sits directly behind it. A few minutes across, scramble down into a gap slicing across the neck of the rock. Ravines now fall away on either side of you. Notice also the pinnacle of rock bursting up on your right. All fours are needed, if you really want to explore. *The way is vertiginous and potentially dangerous from here on!* Scant remains of stone walls appear — part of a medieval CHATEAU (**2h**) that once belonged to the Counts of Cinarca. And what a view you have: you 'hang' straight out over the Gravona Plain and look towards Ajaccio's gulf. Watch the swifts swooping in and out and the lizards hunting, before you return the same way to **Appietto** (**3h30min**).

# 3 FORET DOMANIALE DE CHIAVARI

**See also photograph page 15**

**Distance/time:** 9km/5.6mi; 2h20min (11km/6.8mi; 3h with detour)

**Grade:** easy walk on forestry tracks and trails; overall ascent of 150m/ 500ft (or 200m/650ft if you include the detour from the old prison)

**Equipment:** walking shoes/trainers, bathing things; *IGN map 4153 OT*

**Access:** 🚌 or 🚐 (Timetable 6) to/from Verghia. Motorists can park at the signposted forestry footpath on the D55, 1km east of Verghia (on the north side of the Ruisseau de Zirione). Travelling by bus, alight at Verghia and walk back along the D55 for 10min to the Zirione bridge.

**Short walk/picnic suggestion: Sentier du Myrte** (2.5km/1.5mi; 45min; easy). This signposted forestry circuit through maquis and a cork oak wood (photograph page 15) is waymarked with wooden posts bearing a myrtle leaf motif (one of the constituents of the maquis). Keep left at a fork 10min uphill. After crossing a stream, the path passes an old mill: this is a lovely picnic spot, but there are also benches under the trees.

T his walk takes you through a magnificent forest of cork trees, kermes and holm oaks, eucalyptus and maquis, to Chiavari's old prison. Birdsong accompanies you throughout the walk, which ends on the lovely nature trail in the intimate cork oak wood shown on page 15.

**The walk starts** at the PARKING AREA for the nature trail (Sentier du Myrte) on the north side of the bridge over the **Ruisseau de Zirione**. Walk south over the bridge and after 100m/yds, turn left uphill on a forestry track. Ignore any forks to the right, and you'll come to a T-JUNCTION in a clearing (**15min**). Turn right uphill here (the level track to the left is followed later, when you return from the prison).

You pass a small fenced-in GRAVEYARD on the right (**35min**); continue straight ahead at the junction a couple

*A lovely 'avenue' of eucalyptus trees (top left) leads you to the grim old Chiavari Prison (bottom left). The prison's water supply building (top right) is still visible, and the building where gunpowder was made is some 300m north, on the D55.*

of minutes later. The track widens into a grand 'avenue' bordered with eucalyptus trees, and you soon come to the D55. Across the road is the **Ancien Penitencier de Chiavari (1h)**.

The history of the prison is as grim as the building itself. Of the 200 original prisoners in 1855, 82 per cent died in the first year, due chiefly to the poor hygienic conditions. Later the prison had up to 800 inmates, who worked the land nearby. Many were able to escape, usually with the help of the local people. The prison was closed in 1906. If you have time, you can take a 40-minute detour here (see purple line on the map), just to enjoy the woodlands and birdsong (up to 60 species of birds have been identified in this area).

When you've had your fill of history and nature, return to the track by which you arrived (be sure not to take the higher, motorable track which runs parallel with it for some 200m). Return through the arching eucalyptus and past the cemetery, back down to the junction first encountered at the 15min-point (**1h30min**). Turn right here on the level track, and contour through the shady valleys. A little over half an hour along, ignore a clear path down to the left. Just past this, there is a Forestry Department wooden marker post on the right of the track, quickly followed by one on the left. At this point you can see across the Zirione Valley and have a view down left to the Anse Ottioni, the bay where you set out. About four minutes later, beyond another marker, you come to a junction, where two paths go left downhill (the track continues inland, but ends in about eight minutes). Take either path down to the **Ruisseau de Zirione (2h10min)**.

After crossing the stream on stepping-stones, way-marks on the far side take you curling up left, and you join the **Sentier du Myrte** in a few minutes. Up to the right is an old ruined mill. Turn left on this nature trail* and, at a junction by a marker post with a myrtle leaf motif, keep right, to cross another little stream. Rise up to a crossing path, where there is an electricity pylon over to the right; keep left here, back to the CAR PARK on the D55 (**2h20min**).

*Or, to see more of the nature trail, turn *right* here, pass the old mill, and follow the marker posts back to your car (the Short walk in reverse).

# 4 FORET DOMANIALE DE VIZZAVONA

**Distance/time:** 8.5km/5.3mi; 3h50min (add 1h if travelling by train)
**Grade:** moderate-strenuous, with some short steep scrambles. Ascent of 450m/1475ft. Can be very cold and *dangerous when wet*.
**Equipment:** as page 50; walking boots and bathing things recommended; *IGN map 4251 OT*
**Access:** 🚗, 🚌 (Timetable 21) or 🚐 (Timetable 7) to/from Vizzavona. Travelling by car or bus park/alight almost opposite 'A Muntagnera', an *auberge* 400m east of the Col de Vizzavona on the N193. From the railway station, turn right uphill on the road, to the signposted 'Sentier des Cascades' (also the 'GR20 Nord') — on the right, just before a chapel. *Carefully* follow the red and white GR waymarking (and wooden posts with a pine tree motif) to the bridge over the Agnone, cross it, and pick up the main walk at the 15min-point (add 30min to all times).

**Short walks/picnic suggestions**
**1 Cascades des Anglais** (easy; ascents of about 100m/330ft). Either follow the Sentier des Cascades from the railway station and back (see above; 5km/3mi; 1h30min), or follow the main walk to the 30min-point and back (3.4km/2mi; 1h). Picnic at the *cascades*, in shade or sun.
**2 Ruined fort** (4km/2.5mi; 1h05min *from A Muntagnera;* moderate, but you must be sure-footed; walking boots recommended). Follow the main walk to the 30min-point, then take the path on the left (cairn). This heads back southeast above the GR, contouring through a cairned rock chaos and then beech woods. In 15min, at a Y-fork, turn right, up to the top of the ridge and the ruined fort shown below (2min). Follow the good path (yellow waymarks) east along the ridge, but fork right after a few minutes, down to the N193. Turn left, back to 'A Muntagnera'.

T he cascading Agnone River is the essence of this walk. It bounds down a valley of rock into deep emerald-green pools. Monte d'Oro (2389m/7835ft), Corsica's fifth highest peak, dominates the valley. An apron of pines stretches around its lower slopes, but the valley itself is

*Idyllic picnic spots: the Cascades des Anglais (left) and the ruined fort above the Col de Vizzavona (middle; Short walk 2). Right: Monte d'Oro*

the home of a splendid beech forest. Of all these beautiful gifts of nature, it's the river you'll remember ... and the dazzling Cascades des Anglais.

**The walk begins** almost opposite the *auberge* 'A MUN-TAGNERA'. Follow the track downhill. Monte d'Oro soon appears through the beech trees, filling in this picture. Its naked rocky crown rises high above the pine wood patching its inclines. When the track makes a U-bend down to the right, keep straight ahead on a path — to the crystal-clear, bubbly river, with its green and alluring pools. There is a BRIDGE here, and a seasonal KIOSK (**15min**). The GR20 from Vizzavona crosses the bridge here, while the nature trail keeps to the north side of the river.

Remaining on the south side of the river, we now follow the GR. There is no single clearly-trodden path, so watch out for the red and white waymarks. The Agnone bounces down the valley alongside you, one falls after another — the **Cascades des Anglais**. At the top of the last cascade, a large CAIRN (**30min**) on the left alerts you to an another route back to A Muntagnera (*Short walk 2*).

The route is very steep at times; sometimes you'll be using all fours. Green lichen illuminates the surrounding rock; under direct sunlight it glows with the fluorescence of a highlighter pen. Ignore a turn-off to the left at the **Bergeries de Porteto**, then cross the river on a FOOTBRIDGE (**1h40min**), above a small but thundering waterfall. When you come to the scant remains of the old French Alpine Club (CAF) REFUGE (**2h**), the spring snow-line is not far out of reach. Just below this small crumbled rock shelter is the largest waterfall in the valley. You're completely encircled by mountains — the Monte Renoso chain may still be wearing a mantle of snow.

The walk ends here at the refuge. (If you have time, you might like to continue on the GR20, or climb Monte d'Oro to a viewpoint over the tiny, hidden Lac d'Oro. These strenuous paths are only recommended for experienced hikers who have the relevant IGN map.)

Heading back, don't miss the beryl-green pools in the valley floor; some are magnificent. But if you decide to swim, make sure the pools are safe before you hurl yourself into them; the current can be very strong. Return to the kiosk at the BRIDGE in 1h30min (**3h30min**), then retrace your steps to **A Muntagnera** (**3h50min**). Or cross the bridge and follow the GR/nature trail to **Vizzavona** (**4h 15min**), where the railway station is just downhill to the left or you can catch a bus 10 minutes uphill to the right.

## 5  BERGERIES DE TOLLA

**Distance/time:** 9km/5.6mi; 2h55min

**Grade:** fairly easy, with an ascent/descent of 290m/950ft, but not advisable in bad weather.

**Equipment:** as page 50 (sturdy shoes will suffice), bathing things; *IGN map 4251 OT*

**Access:** 🚗 to/from Canaglia (via the D23, about 5km south of Vivario). Or 🚂 to/from Tattone (Timetable 21; adds 3.5km/1h each way). From the station platform, head north along the railway tracks in the direction of Corte. Some 140m/yds along, cross the tracks and follow the level path that disappears into the pines (handwritten sign: 'Canaglia, GR20'). This takes you to the D23, where you turn left.

*Cascade du Meli*

**Short walk/picnic suggestion: Manganello River** (3km/2mi; 55min). Follow the main walk to the 25min-point; return the same way. Ample shade; boulders to sit on.

I first did this walk in autumn, and what a splendour awaited me. The beech trees left me in awe with their golds and yellows. The streams and rivers were magnificent cascades, filled by the autumn rains. Deep in the valley a wisp of smoke curling above the trees led me to the Bergerie de Tolla, a lonely pastoral outpost. Entering it was like walking into a children's story book.

**The walk starts** at **Canaglia**, a small hamlet high on a hillside between the pine forest and chestnut trees, overlooking the confluence of the Manganello and Vecchio rivers. Three tracks face you here: take the track on the right, signposted 'BERGERIE DE TOLLA 1H15MIN', to head up into the valley. High rocky summits peer above the thickly-wooded walls. You pass a HORSE CORRAL. When the track forks on the far side of a bridge (**5-6min**), follow the orange flash waymarking of the Mare a Mare Nord down to the right (signpost: 'VERS GR 20'). Pass a faint fork off to the right and come to the narrow, thundering **Manganello River** (**25min**). (Swimmers: take the strong current into account.) The way narrows here, and alders grow along the riverside.

After about an hour of gentle uphill walking, you round a bend, to see the **Cascade du Meli** on the left (**1h20min**; see photograph page 63), and a bridge takes you over its cascading waters. The higher you climb, the more striking the colours become, especially in the beech forest up ahead. Not long after passing the waterfall, leave this path and cross the Manganello on the **Passerelle de Tolla**, following a signpost for the 'BERGERIE DE TOLLA'. (On your return from the *bergerie*, provided you're not all puffed out, I do recommend wandering up the path to the left signposted to the 'REFUGE DE L'ONDA', for about 35 minutes. In autumn it's a must! You'll soon find yourself in a dense wood where moss coats the trees and drips off the rocks. It could be a Japanese garden.)

The **Grottaccia River** joins the Manganello just where you cross it. Once again you'll be reaching for your camera, to capture the Manganello as it surges out of a rocky gorge leaving swirling beryl-green pools in its wake. The best swimming hole is just a couple of minutes downstream from the bridge. Once over the river, your

*The Bergeries de Tolla. These small stone dwellings in a grassy clearing create a setting straight out of a book of fairy tales. Watch out for the mischievous donkeys here. They wander over to greet you, full of innocence, and just as you try to slip past, they reach for a nibble of your … you know what!*

waymarking changes to the red and white flashes of the GR20. The livestock have created their own trails here, so be sure to follow the waymarks carefully. Don't forget to look behind you: high on the mountainside you'll spot a beech wood, a spectacular fire of colours in autumn.

Heading through a gap in the hills, you enter an enclosed valley and stumble upon the 'story book' **Bergeries de Tolla (1h35min)**. In season you can usually get a light meal here. For most of you this will be far enough. However, even more spectacular scenery lies further up the valley. (You could continue for another 50 minutes, or until you reach a log bridge crossing the river to your left, from where you look straight up into a cascade that leaps and bounds down the valley wall. To get there, take the path to the right of the last house at the *bergerie*.)

Return the same way to **Canaglia (2h55min)** or the railway station at Tattone (4h55min), but don't forget to add on ample extra time if you continue up the GR20 beyond the *bergerie* or you take the detour towards the Refuge de l'Onda.

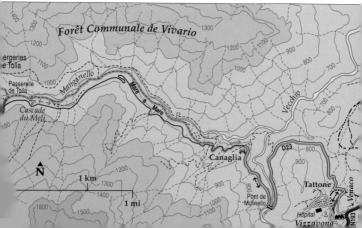

## 6 PONTE DI NOCETA

**Distance/time:** 12km/7.5mi; 4h15min

**Grade:** moderate, with overall ascents/descents of 450m/1475ft. You must be sure-footed and have a head for heights. Steep, gravelly path beyond Zucchero; dangerous if wet. Don't attempt the walk in changeable weather.

**Equipment:** as page 50; walking boots, warm clothing, bathing things recommended; *IGN maps 4251 OT, 4351 OT*

**Access:** 🚗 (park at the railway station), 🚌 (Timetable 21) or 🚐 (Timetable 7) to/from Venaco

**Short walk/picnic suggestion: Ponte di Noceta**. Access by 🚗: the bridge lies on the D43, southeast of Venaco. Plenty of shade, boulders to sit on. Follow the waymarked path west along the Vecchio River for as long as you like.

A n inviting pool awaits the swimmer; a profusion of spring flowers greets the botanist; superb scenery entices the photographer; the Vecchio lures the fisherman. But for all that, I'm sorry to say that if you take the absolutely spectacular train ride to Venaco, the walk may be a bit of an anti-climax!

**Begin the walk** at the RAILWAY STATION in **Venaco**. Follow the railway line north towards Lugo, and branch off left into the trees on a stone-laid path 150m/yds along (about 100m before the railway goes into a tunnel). Once in **Lugo (8min)**, follow the village lane downhill to the right. A circle of high ink-coloured hills is seen in the distance. Venaco sits across the valley in the shadows of a towering wall of grey rock. At the end of the village, and now on a path, come to a wooden cross and orange flashes waymarking the route. Veer left and head down into the valley, passing plots and fruit trees. Cross a tiny BRIDGE in a few minutes and, at a fork 50m/yds further on, go left. Ascending now, you enjoy a fine view of Venaco. Soon two short stretches of path may prove un-nerving for less experienced walkers.

Rounding the ridge (**45min**), you come to the local incinerator. Your route

66

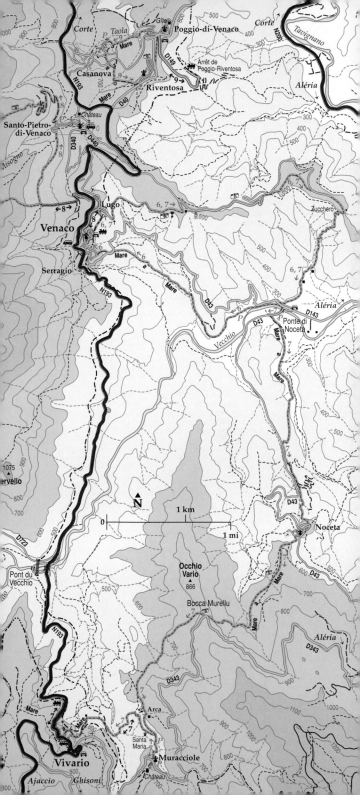

swings up sharply left here: you cross the crest of the ridge and meet a road. Follow it to the right (orange flashes, signs: 'PONTE DI NOCETA, ZUCCHERU', soon passing the transmitter station. As the road mounts the ridge, you look down into the wide-open Tavignano Valley. Some 2km along the road, about 20-30m *beyond* a sharp bend to the left, turn off right on a short-cut path (orange waymark). Two more short-cuts follow: *watch carefully for the orange waymarks.* You drop down to the outpost of **Zucchero** (**1h40min**). From here descend a waymarked path on the right, down into the maquis-matted valley. Less than 100m/yds down, fork off sharp left; a little further on, an arrow indicates that the way swings back again, to the right. *This gravelly path drops rapidly. Take special care if it's at all damp.*

You cross a stream near a slate-roofed cottage (**2h 20min**). Eight minutes later, pass a derelict farmstead. Soon reach the D43, and turn left, alongside the noisy **Vecchio River**. Some 100m/yds along, you pass the turn-off right back to Venaco, but for the moment, continue to the **Ponte di Noceta** (**2h30min**), for a swim and a picnic.

Return to the signpost for Venaco and follow the path beside the river (orange flashes of the Mare a Mare Nord), joining an old track 15 minutes along. Eight minutes later, when the track swings sharply up to the right, continue straight ahead alongside a stone wall. Ignore all branch-offs. Beyond a stream crossing, you rise for a little over 1km. When you meet the D43 again, follow it to the left for 75m/yds, then turn right uphill on a waymarked lane. At a T-junction in **Venaco**, turn right downhill for the train or left uphill and left again for the bus: flag it down on the main N193 (**4h15min**).

*A delightful deep pool awaits you here at the Ponte di Noceta.*

# 7 FROM VENACO TO VIVARIO

**See map pages 66-67**

**Distance/time:** 21km/13mi; 7h35min (8h if travelling by train)

**Grade:** strenuous (overall ascents of 900m/2950ft, descents of 800m/2625ft). Short but steep, gravelly descent to Zucchero; long ascent of 580m/1900ft to the Bocca Murellu. You must be sure-footed and have a head for heights. *Dangerous if wet;* don't attempt in changeable weather.

**Equipment:** as page 50; walking boots, warm clothing, bathing things recommended; *IGN maps 4251 OT, 4351 OT*

**Access:** 🚌 (Timetable 21) or 🚐 (Timetable 7) to Venaco; return on the same train or bus from Vivario

**Short walk/picnic suggestion: Vivario — Muracciole — Vivario** (6.5km/4mi; 1h50min; easy, with overall descents/ascents of 260m/850ft; walking boots recommended). 🚌, 🚐 (Timetable 8) or 🚌 (Timetable 21) to Vivario. From the large fountain with the bronze statue in Vivario walk north downhill towards Corte on the N193. A minute along (just before the bar-glacier), turn right down concrete steps (signpost: 'Chapelle d'Arca, Muracciole'; orange flash of the Mare a Mare Nord). Just past the back of the school, turn left down a concrete lane. Pass a house on the left, ignore a path turning sharply left downhill, and keep right down a cart track. Cross the railway on a bridge (10min) and 2min later turn right on a path in front of the gate to a house. This narrow path descends in pitch-black shade. Cross the railway again (20min; cairn), then cross a stream on slippery stepping stones (25min). After recrossing the stream a minute later, the path curls left up hillside. Ascending in deep shade, *carefully* watch for the orange waymarks (and cairns) on this convoluted path, as you pass through ruins and beside stone walls. You pass to the left of the Chapelle Santa Maria (40min) and descend to a creepered bridge three minutes later. Beyond the bridge, climb up to Muriaccole, keeping left at all forks. Return the same way. The best picnic spot is near Muriaccole's church or, on a hot day, down by the bridge just below Muriacciole. Return the same way.

Traipsing along and over ridges, you cross unkempt hills foraged by a handful of cows and goats; otherwise you're likely to have little company on these old trails linking six Venachese villages.

**Begin** by following WALK 6 to the **Ponte di Noceta (2h30min)**, shown opposite. Cross the bridge and follow the D43 west for 200m/yds, then turn left on a farm track (orange waymarks of the Mare a Mare Nord). A few minutes up the track, branch off right on a path. At the fork eight minutes along, keep right for Noceta. (There are two paths turning off to the right here, one just before the small shady stream, the other running alongside it. Take the latter.) A little over ten minutes further on, the route turns right uphill between stone walls (just before twin telephone poles), to climb up to the D43. Turn left on the road for a little over 150m/yds, then turn off left, on a track signposted for 'NOCETA'. When you reach a fork within five minutes, bear right uphill; 50m/yds along, bear right again, on a rough path.

*Bocca Murellu. The longest climb in the hike rises to this pass — a steady pull of 580m from the Ponte di Noceta.*

Entering **Noceta (4h10min)**, keep south uphill on the D43. Many old mountain villages like Noceta have undergone a transformation and are once again inhabited. A couple of minutes uphill you come to a FOUNTAIN and a charming old CHURCH. Head up the lane to the right of the church. Some 200m/yds uphill turn left on a path (signs: 'VIVARIO', 'MURACCIOLE'. Keep right at the next fork. You cross an unused track a couple of times. Your panorama now extends across to the Venaco side of the valley. In spring a great profusion of flowers entertains you with its colours — blue, indigo, yellow, pink, and white.

Crossing the **Bocca Murellu** (824m/2700ft; **5h15min**), you're soon following an old mule track. Vivario comes into sight, ahead to your left, stretching across a wooded hillside. Monte d'Oro (Walk 4) rises sharply in the background. Keep left at the next two junctions. Muracciole lies ahead, crowned by its miniature château. Some 400m/yds beyond the enchanting, crumbled hamlet of **Arca**, a WAYMARKED PATH joins from the right (**6h05min**). But keep ahead: cross a small BRIDGE draped in creepers and climb into **Muracciole** (**6h30min**). The place has a timeless air; it exudes charm. The château rises behind the FOUNTAIN, which is shaded by a fragrant lime tree.

Making for Vivario, return to BRIDGE and keep left at the Y-fork beyond it. In three minutes pass to the right of the solitary **Chapelle Santa Maria**. Watch the orange waymarks carefully on the next stretch, as you pass crumbled buildings and walls. You slide down into a narrow valley in deep shade, crossing two streams. In spring, cyclamen shed some light in these pitch-black woods.

Fifty minutes from Muracciole you cross the railway. A wide path takes you up through a thin wood. Soon you join a track. A steep 10-minute climb sees you in **Vivario** (**7h35min**). The BUS STOP lies a minute uphill to the left, on the N193, in front of the FOUNTAIN WITH A BRONZE STATUE. (If it's Sunday or a holiday, you'll have to catch the train. The station is 1km north downhill: take the first left turn.)

## 8 SANTO-PIETRO-DI-VENACO CIRCUIT

**See map pages 66-67**
**Distance/time:** 11km/6.8mi; 5h

**Grade:** strenuous ascent and very steep descent of 850m/ 2790ft. You must be sure-footed, with a head for heights. *Less experienced walkers should descend from the Santo Eliseo chapel by the ascent route. Do not attempt in changeable weather.*

**Equipment:** as page 50; walking

boots, sunhat and warm clothing recommended; *IGN map 4251 OT*

**Access:** 🚗 to/from Santo-Pietro-di-Venaco: park by the church. There is also a 🚌 (Timetable 7) to/from Santo-Pietro or 🚂 to/from Venaco (Timetable 21).

**Short walk/picnic suggestion:** Follow the main walk a short way (garden, nature trail); allow 1h.

*Photo: Bergerie de Tatarellu*

High on mountainside shelves you discover blissfully quiet pastoral outposts *(bergeries)* surrounded by lush grass. Cold mountain streams crash down the gullies around you, and your views expand with every step.

**Start the walk** at the CHURCH and FOUNTAIN (with walkers' SIGNBOARD) in **Santo-Pietro**. Follow the road at the right of the church. At a fork, go right for 'COTO PRATU', crossing a bridge (left is the return route). Your track (initially tarred and marked with orange flashes) zigzags up through dense oak woods. About 2km uphill, leave the track: take a steep path to the left. You'll pass a shepherds' shelter: peek inside, to see how the rocks are layered and how cosy this igloo-like structure is. Once out of the scrub, a magnificent view quenches your scenic thirst: you look southeast over the confluence of the Vecchio and Tavignano valleys.

The ground is cushioned in moss as you near the alpine zone. Beyond a fork (keep right) you come to the **Chapelle Santo Eliseo (2h30min)** and a *bergerie*. A sheer rock wall ahead seals off the interior of the island; streams gallop down on either side of the ridge.

Rising gently, you cross two streams, before gaining a small plateau and the **Bergerie de Codopratu (3h20min)**. The path crosses another stream and later contours round the hillside. After 1km, you are looking straight down into the Vecchio Valley, and the descent begins. *It's very steep and requires the utmost concentration.* The **Bergerie de Tatarellu**, sheltering up against a beech tree grove on slopes illuminated by hellebores, is but a brief pause in this rocketing descent. Be sure to fork right for 'VENACO' not far past the last hut, *keeping a careful eye on the waymarks.* When you come to a SIGNPOSTED T-JUNCTION, go left, back down to **Santo-Pietro (5h)**. (Or, if you've come by train, turn right downhill to Venaco.)

# 9 CIRCUIT FROM POGGIO-DI-VENACO

**See map pages 66-67; see also photograph page 4**
**Distance/time:** 3km/2mi; 50min
**Grade:** easy ups and downs
**Equipment:** as page 50; stout shoes recommended; IGN map 4251 OT
**Access:** 🚍 to/from Poggio-

di-Venaco (D40 north of Venaco), or 🚌 to/from Poggio-Riventosa (Timetable 21; add 45min)
**Picnic: Ruisseau de Taola** (20min)
*Left: detail on a tomb in Poggio; below: Ruisseau de Taola*

This short circuit of three villages is a gem. Mostly in shade, it takes you out past a burbling stream and back with superb views over the way you've come and to Corte and the surrounding bowl of mountains.

Start out in **Poggio**: with your back to the WAR MEMORIAL, walk down the road narrow ahead, at the right of an electricity transformer (sign: 'CASANOVA, CORTE'; orange flash of the Mare a Mare Nord on an electricity pole at the right). You pass below a CEMETERY on the left (**2min**). When the road makes a U-turn to the right (**4min**), go left downhill on a path (orange flash). Cross a burbling stream on a FOOTBRIDGE and rise up through a ferny dell. Approaching Casanova, veer right on a cart track and walk to the left of a stone hut. You come to the end of a road, which you will follow to the left uphill. But first walk down to the **Ruisseau de Taola** (**20min**): either go straight along the cart track to a dam, or take a path half-right, just where the road begins.

The road passes a camp site on the left and a FOUNTAIN on the right, as you skirt **Casanova**, with its traditional slate-roofed buildings. Go straight over a crossroads, onto a cobbled path and, almost at once, turn left on a crossing path. Rise up to a road and cross it (**25min**). Ignore a track to the left (by a TOMB with cypresses) and keep ahead towards Riventosa, which rises above to left, spread out along a ridge. Contour through tall grass, then cross another tinkling stream on a FOOTBRIDGE (**30min**) and pass the **Moulin de Riventosa** on the right. A shady track takes you up to **Riventosa**. Pass to the right of the CEMETERY, then continue to the right uphill on a concrete road. Reaching the main D40 (**40min**; TAP, WAR MEMORIAL), walk up the cobbled road, at the right of the CHURCH. At a Y-fork, go right on a narrow road (tremendous view towards Corte). Back on the D40, turn left and, after 30m/yds, fork right on a footpath. This widens to a lane running above the road to the railway, and takes you back to **Poggio** (**50min**).

# 10  EVISA TO OTA (SPELUNCA GORGE)

See also photographs on pages 12 and 76
**Distance/time:** 7km/4.3mi; 2h25min

**Grade:** fairly easy, with a steep (although not difficult) descent of 620m/ 2030ft and ascent of 130m/425ft. Slippery in wet weather.

**Equipment:** as page 50; walking boots, bathing things recommended; *IGN map 4150 OT*

**Access:** 🚌 to Evisa (Timetable 3); return by 🚌 from Ota (Timetable 2)

**Short walks/picnic suggestions: Ponte Vecchiu or Pont de Zaglia** (up to 3km/2mi; 1h; easy; photographs overleaf). Access by 🚗: Park near 'les Deux Ponts d'Ota', on the D124 below Ota. You can see the Ponte Vecchiu as you descend from Ota; picnic there (20min return) or follow the orange waymarks east along the Spelunca Gorge and picnic by the Genoese Pont de Zaglia (35min each way). Shade, swimming holes.

The Spelunca Gorge is a must for every visitor. Imposing buttresses of pink- to violet-hued rock bursting up out of the valley dominate the landscape. Deep in the gorge, you wander alongside a tumbling river, crossed by old arched footbridges. In summer you'll be tempted to swim in one of the inviting pools. The walk ends at the delightful village of Ota, in majestic countryside.

You'll spend more time on buses getting to and from the walk than actually walking ... but the journey is through such superb landscapes that you can look forward to a 'perfect day'. **Start the walk** in **Evisa**, a high mountain village in a cloak of chestnut trees. Follow the road back downhill towards Porto for about 10 minutes, until you reach the END OF THE CEMETERY and a SIGN DENOTING THE VILLAGE EXIT. Already you will have noticed the rose-tinted granite peaks rising up out of the landscape.

A large signpost for 'SPELUNCA', on the right, indicates your path. It is paved initially and waymarked with the orange flashes of the Tra Mare e Monti. You dip down into a maquis wood sprinkled with pines, through which you can see the hillside village of Ota with its red-tiled roofs. Pink crags overshadow it. In the distance, the valley winds down to the sea. This old mule trail (slippery when wet) descends very steeply. Moss coats the surrounding trees, and the banks are flecked with cyclamen. Looking back, to the right, you see a bald mound of shiny grey rock bulging out of the summits. Soon precipitous, scrub-covered walls tower above you. Reaching the valley floor, you cross a stream on the beautifully-cobbled Genoese **Pont de Zaglia** (**1h10min**), shaded by alders. The stream joins a fast-flowing river just below the bridge, and you may be tempted to swim. Soon the Capu di Larata (1193m/3915ft), Ota's guardian, holds your attention.

Crossing the D124 (**1h45min**), take the concrete lane

73

off left, down into the valley floor (some 80m/yds *before* a couple of pretty stone bridges, **les Deux Ponts d'Ota**). Circle to the right of a football pitch, soon rejoining the river. A little over 10 minutes along, you cross the river on the **Ponte Vecchiu**, a perfectly-restored Genoese footbridge. The pool below is ideal for swimming.

Over the bridge, swing left and follow the right bank of the river. Two mountains thrusting up from the valley ahead steal your attention. As you climb amidst swirls of grasshoppers, houses appear, stepped one behind the other on the hillside. Once on the main street in **Ota** (**2h25min**), turn left. The bus leaves from a turning area by a FOUNTAIN on the right, 100m/yds east of the post office. But first look around, read the dates above the doors, and absorb the wonderful atmosphere of this charming, superbly-sited village set below towering pink rock walls, amidst olive and fruit trees.

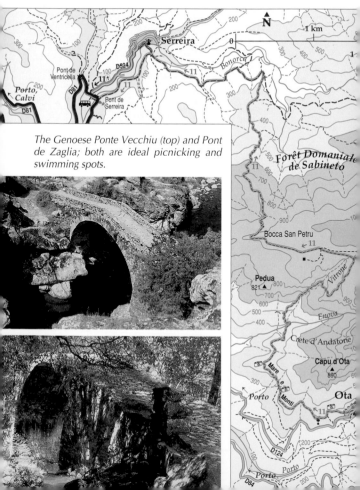

*The Genoese Ponte Vecchiu (top) and Pont de Zaglia; both are ideal picnicking and swimming spots.*

# 11 FROM OTA TO SERRIERA

**See also photographs on pages 2 and 12**

**Distance/time:** 12.5km/7.75mi; 5h

**Grade:** strenuous, with an ascent of 560m/1835ft at the start, much of it very steep. The descent (875m/2870ft) is also very steep, and dangerous if wet. You must be sure-footed and have a head for heights.

**Equipment:** as page 50; walking boots, sun protection, bathing things recommended; *IGN map 4150 OT*

**Access:** 🚌 to Ota (Timetable 2). Return on the same bus from *Porto*. In high season (15/5-15/10) you can catch a bus to Porto on the D81 at the Serriera turn-off (Timetable 8); otherwise you will have to walk (add 1h40min), or arrange for a taxi. *NB*: If you're based at Ajaccio, this walk demands an overnight stay in Porto. In peak season, reserve accommodation well in advance.

You set out overlooking the luxuriant, tree-smothered Porto Valley, and you end up in a landscape of dark rolling hills. In between, the route clambers up through a gap in the hills, where lofty, rose-coloured rock walls look down on you. All along the way you catch glimpses of the stunning Porto Gulf, of pink granite sea-bluffs, secluded coves and deep blue sea.

**The walk begins** in **Ota**, where the bus turns round by a FOUNTAIN (100m/yds east of the POST OFFICE). Fill your bottles with water, then climb the wide old stone-paved mule trail. It's a section of the 'Mare e Monti' route, so is marked with orange paint. The way becomes a concrete lane but, after swinging up behind the last houses, you're on the trail again. (A short stretch of path some 15 minutes along may prove difficult for inexperienced walkers.)

Superb views encompass you. Already high up, you look straight across the valley. Chestnut groves sprinkled across the slopes cheer up the dark countryside. Before you head around the hillside, take a moment to look back at Ota, with its bright orange-tiled rooftops and bib of grey-green olive trees. Soon Porto comes into view, trickling down to the sea alongside the final stretch of the Porto River. At the end of the village you can see a rock crowned with an ancient tower jutting into the sea (photograph pages 10-11). Minutes later, go right at the junction.

Mounting a RIDGE (**50min**), you look over into a narrow side-valley, where walls of rose-coloured rock seem to block your way. Looking back, you soon catch a glimpse of Porto's picture-postcard beach. Troupes of pink-

*Ota, superbly sited below towering rock walls*

flowering foxgloves flourish on rubble-strewn patches of hillside. Zigzagging back into this 'pink' valley, you scramble up through a narrow gap in rock walls, where the scent of the pale mauve-to-blue rosemary plants may surround you. When the path swings sharply uphill to the left, near the edge of the ridge (**2h20min**), there is a fine outlook over Porto's valley just to the right: the dome-shaped Capu d'Orto (Walk 15) dominates the landscape. Continuing up through pines and heather, you come into a spacious chestnut grove. A SPRING is passed en route, and then a small stone building, up on the rocky hillock of **Pedua** to the left.

From here the path rises gently to a signposted pass (**Bocca San Petru**; **3h**). A nearly-vertical descent follows … possibly on your backside. The countryside ahead eases out into smooth rolling hills but, inland, peaks still capped with snow appear in the distance. Further down-hill, you spot the striking Bussaglia Beach, sprawling across the mouth of the wide, gravelly bed of the Vetricella River.

Clambering down a rocky ridge, you soon look straight down onto Serriera (**3h20min**). The village is as red as the hillside rock from which it was built. Pass through a lovely glade and then come out onto a track. Remain on this track for 50 minutes, all the way to the MAIN PORTO ROAD (D81; **5h**).(Or follow the 'Mare e Monti' into **Serriera**, then walk along the D524 to the D81.) There is a bus stop at the junction of the D524 and D81 (near the restored fountain shown on page 2).

# 12 CASCADES D'AITONE

**Distance/time:** 3.2km/2mi; 1h10min

**Grade:** easy, but you must be agile. Descent/ascent of 70m/230ft.

**Equipment:** as page 50; strong shoes and bathing things recommended; *IGN map 4150 OT*

**Access:** 🚗 to/from a parking area *just below the track to the Aitone Forestry house,* on the north side of the D84 between Evisa and the Col de Vergio. (There are *two* parking areas for the cascades: park at the higher one, *not* by the fire-point sign 'EVI05'.)

**Picnic suggestion: Piscine d'Aitone** (2.3km/1.5mi; 40min; easy). Follow the main walk for 20min and return the same way. Shade; picnic tables.

**Alternative walk: Sentier de la Sittelle** (3.2km/2mi; 1h; easy, very little ascent). This Forestry Department nature trail lies about 2.5km north of the Cascades trail, just north of two 'Paisolu d'Aitone' signs (large parking area). It is waymarked with wooden posts bearing a bird motif (the *sittelle: Sitta Whiteheadi,* the Corsican nuthatch). Beautiful walk through Corsican pines and fir trees; picnic tables by the Aitone. See map.

Long a favourite spot for trout fishermen and swimmers, up until 1905 the Cascades d'Aitone also powered three mills for grinding chestnut flour — once a staple of the local diet. This short walk is a delight of waterfalls glistening through a mixed wood of pine, fir, yew and beech.

**Start out** by taking the forestry track at the SIGNPOST and fork sharp left downhill after about 150m/yds (a right goes to the forestry house). Descend gently to a picnic area with tables, where the Mare a Mare Nord comes in from a track on the left. Steps take you down to the **Piscine d'Aitone (20min)**, a good picnicking and swimming spot.

Stay on the left (south) side of the **Ruisseau d'Aitone** and follow the rough path (agility required) beside the cascading river as far as the signpost 'FIN DE SENTIER BALISÉE'. From here you have a fine view of the largest waterfall, the **Cascade de la Valla Scarpa (35min)**. One of the mills stood here; now there are only some walls and two millstones. Return the same way, passing two more ruined mills, to the PARKING AREA on the D84 (**1h10min**).

# 13  LE CHATEAU-FORT

See map page 81; see also photograph page 13
**Distance/time:** 1.5km/1mi; 1h
**Grade:** easy, but with many ups and downs, clambering over rock
**Equipment:** as page 50; *IGN map 4150 OT*
**Access:** 🚗 to/from the Tête de Chien (D81, 6.5km north of Piana)

This short walk (with many picnic places) is characterised by whimsical rock formations and superb vistas over les Calanche and the Porto Gulf — from the tower all the way to the Gulf of Girolata.

**The walk begins** at the **Tête de Chien** (PARKING AREA, SIGNPOST; photograph page 12); it's waymarked (in pale green at time of writing) and well trodden. It descends at first, then undulates along a ridge and rises to a ROCKY PLATFORM (**30min**) looking out to the '**Château-Fort**', a castle-like rock pillar rising sheer from the valley below.

Return the same way to the PARKING AREA (**1h**).

# 14 LES CALANCHE

**See map page 81**
**Distance/time:** up to 3.5km/2.2mi; 1h35min (just 1h 05min by bus)
**Grade:** generally easy ups and downs (100m/ 300ft in all), but there is some clambering, requiring agility
**Equipment:** as page 50; sunhat recommended; *IGN map 4150 OT*

**Access:** as Walk 15, page 80
**Alternative walk:** Three extensions north to/from the *very busy* D81 are possible (purple lines on the map), one is almost opposite Walk 13.
**Picnic suggestion:** There are lovely spots all along, but the only good shade on the mule trail is at the 50min-point.

This short ramble is a brilliant introduction to les Calanche and an ideal leg-stretcher for motorists. We follow the old mule trail between Piana and Ota. While much of it has succumbed to the D81, a good stretch of the beautiful stone-laid route still survives.

**The walk begins** at the **Pont de Mezzanu** (PARKING). Just north of the bridge, turn right (east) on a track signposted 'STADE' and 'SENTIERS DE RANDONNÉE'. At a fork 50m/yds along, keep left on a level track (various signposts, including 'ANCIEN CHEMIN DE PIANA A OTA 30MIN'. At the stadium *(stade)*, take the footpath signposted 'PASSERELLE', to walk half-left across the stadium towards more signposts on far side. Cross a FOOTBRIDGE and go left at the signposted fork just beyond it. This clear path is cairned.

On coming to a Y-fork in a small CLEARING (**30min**), keep left to more signposts, then go straight ahead, following 'ANCIEN CHEMIN DE PIANA A OTA'. Now you pick up the old mule trail (photograph above), and it's nothing less than spectacular. Soon after rounding the ridge, you're greeted by mouth-watering views. The wine-coloured arm of Punta Scandola reaches out in the distance, while Piana slumbers in haze. Bits and pieces of the D81 thread their way through the rock pinnacles below.

You'll spot various old waymarks (some green, some blue dots on a white ground), but the path is easily seen. Sometimes you'll need to clamber. If you're planning to picnic, keep your fingers crossed that no one's already taken *the* spot — a large TREE WITH TWO FLAT ROCKS either side (**50min**) — the *only shade* in this wilderness of rock.

Turn back just past here (before the path descends steeply), and retrace your steps to the **Pont de Mezzanu** (**1h35min**). But if you're catching a bus, continue the zigzag descent (slippery when wet) to the D81 and turn right to **les Roches Bleues** (**1h05min**; bar/kiosk).

# 15 CAPU D'ORTO

**See also photographs on pages 12 and 79**

**Distance/time:** 12km/7.4mi; 5h45min (6h05min by bus)

**Grade:** strenuous ascent/descent of 825m/2700ft. The detour to the Capu d'Orto summit at 1294m/4244ft involves some clambering and is only recommended for very experienced, sure-footed hikers with a head for heights. It can be very cold or cloudy on the peak and very dangerous in wet conditions; this walk is only suitable on fine, settled days.

**Equipment:** as page 50; walking boots, sun protection, warm clothing recommended; *IGN map 4150 OT*

**Access:** 🚗 or 🚌 (Timetable 2) to the Pont de Mezzanu, 1km east of Piana. If travelling by bus, *return from les Roches Bleues*.

**Alternative walk: Foce d'Orto** (10km/6.2mi; 4h10min; fairly strenuous, with overall ascents/descents of 700m/2300ft. Follow the main walk to the 1h15min-point. Keep right here and, at the faint fork 15min later, turn left. Eight minutes uphill you're at the Foce d'Orto — a gap in the rock. From here you have wonderful views of the inland hills and the village of Evisa, high on a plateau. Return to the 'Fontaine' junction and continue the main walk, but *ignore* the turn-off for the Capu d'Orto. *A second alternative* is to take the steep cairned path from the Foce d'Orto to the Capu d'Orto (1h) and pick up the main walk at the 2h45min-point.

This walk turns the weird and wonderful weather-sculpted rock of les Calanche inside-out for you. Heading inland from the Calanche, the landscape changes again, and you wind your way around massive mounds of bare pink and grey rock. From the summit of Capu d'Orto you the enjoy five-star views shown below.

*View from the summit of Capu d'Orto. For me, this is the most breathtaking viewpoint on the island. Porto sits far below, the whole gulf lit up by its beach. A rugged coastline twirls its way north, leaving behind small coves.*

**The walk begins** at the **Pont de Mezzanu** (PARKING, BUS STOP). Just north of the bridge, turn right (east) on a track signposted 'STADE' and 'SENTIERS DE RANDONNÉE'. At a fork 50m/yds along, you will see 'Capu d'Orto' signposted to the left. But keep *right* here, following 'CAPU DI U VITULLU'. You enter a V-shaped valley lined with rocky hills and soon pass a RESERVOIR on the left. The inclines on your left are pink; those to the right are grey. Capu di u Vitullu (1330m/4362ft) is the impressive mountain of rock dominating the right-hand side of the valley. Capu d'Orto is still hidden from sight by the ever-billowing mounds of rock on your left. Keep left at the fork (**15min**). When the track ends (**35min**), take the wide cobbled path to the right (SIGNPOST). Heather and strawberry trees flank the way, and the path narrows as you ascend into pines. Within the next 15 minutes, ignore a faint turn-off to the left. Some 25 minutes later you reach a junction where the word 'FONTAINE' (**1h15min**) is carved in a rock. Branch off left here for 'CAPU D'ORTO'. *(But go right uphill for the Alternative walk or if you want to ascend to the Capu d'Orto from the Foce d'Orto.)* Soon bushes of wild rosemary, with their pale blue blooms and strongly-scented leaves, capture your attention. You head across a wooded basin, where the path crosses a stream (usually dry).

At the **Bocca di Piazza Moninca** (**1h40min**) you come to your turn-off right for Capu d'Orto (green waymarks). Now you have to scramble up the rose-coloured rock, brushing through clumps of rosemary and watching out for the waymarking and cairns. Bizzare rock formations *(tafoni)* grow up around you, their colours intensifying. After less than 10 minutes' scrambling, the impressive peak confronts you, bulging straight up out of the landscape. A fine veil of bright green lichen covers the rock face, which is separated from you by a shallow neck of pine-collared rock. Two paths drop down towards the pines; you can use either. Now the real climb begins.

You come to a slight groove in the hillside, where the words 'CAPU D'ORTO' and an ARROW pointing straight up (**2h15min**) appear in faded paint on the rock. From here on the way is marked by a 'museum' of CAIRNS. If you don't enjoy scrambling up a steep rock face (especially with the prospect of getting back down), call it a day here and just lap up the view. The heights of the Calanche bump their way seaward, getting more unruly and expressive as they go. Beyond this realm of pink rock, you see Piana wrapped in greenery, nestling high on a crest.

Those climbing to the summit will find hand-holds a help in tackling this 'groove'. Just when you think you're almost there, the twin-breasted peak looms up ahead … still 25 minutes away! You cross a small grassy shelf and then the final assault begins, again with the help of your hands. *Make sure all the rocks you stand on or lean against are secure!* Once in the cleavage of the split peak, clamber *carefully* up onto the right-hand protrusion — the SUMMIT of **Capu d'Orto** (**2h45min**). The view is the most breath-taking that I have seen on all my walks on Corsica. Not only do you overlook Porto's sweep of beach and tower but, inland, great rounded hills roll back one onto the other. Evisa is seen, set on a plateau back in the hills. To the southwest, the vista stretches as far as the bays of Cargèse — the gulfs of Chiuni and Péru. A little further along to the right, you peer down onto Ota, resting at the foot of an amphitheatre of rose-coloured rock.

Descend back to the **Bocca di Piazza Moninca** (**3h 45min**), and head right, following the green waymarks. At a waymarked junction about five minutes later, keep right. You get another glimpse of Piana, this time framed between rocky outcrops and flowering scrub. Passing through a neat STONE WALL (**4h45min**), the bay reappears through trees. Just below lies a DELL OF CHESTNUTS and pines, where you ignore a turn-off to the right. A few minutes beyond the dell, keep left (green waymarks). Soon you're looking down into the valley you ascended earlier.

Descending through a clearing thick with cistus and heather, you reach SIGNPOSTS (**5h20min**). *If you've come by car,* head *left* here (green and blue waymarks), making sure to follow the path where it cuts back to the left a couple of minutes down. Beyond a FOOTBRIDGE and STADIUM, you're back at the **Pont de Mezzanu** (**5h 45min**). *To catch a bus,* fork right ('ANCIEN CHEMIN DE PIANA A OTA') and follow Walk 14 from the 30min-point (page 79). Flag down a bus at **les Roches Bleues** (**6h05min**).

# 16 CALVI • NOTRE DAME DE LA SERRA • LA REVELLATA • CALVI

**See map on page 84**
**Distance/time:** 8.5km/5.3mi; 2h 10min
**Grade:** fairly easy ascent/descent of 200m/650ft on good tracks and paths
**Equipment:** as page 50; stout shoes, sun protection, bathing wear recommended; *IGN map 4149 OT*
**Access:** The walk begins and ends at Calvi's railway station.
**Longer walk:** la Revellata (15km/9.3mi; 3h40min; grade as main walk). Follow the main walk to the Plage de l'Alga (1h30min), then go *left* on the coastal path. Beyond the

largest cove (Anse de l'Oscelluccia), the path rises and eventually climbs to the road to the lighthouse. Turn right to the lighthouse at the end of the point. From here you can continue 0.5km to the Marine Biology Research Centre: it's private, but access on foot is allowed. If you would like to visit it, arrange this in advance (tel: 04 95 65 06 18; fax 04 95 65 01 34). Return the same way to the Plage d'Alga and pick up the main walk again.
*Photograph: research centre and lighthouse at La Revellata*

T his delightful ramble is best enjoyed late in the day, when you can combine it with an evening picnic at the chapel, watching the fishing boats, yachts and high-speed ferries making for the port below Calvi's citadel.

**Start out** by following WALK 17 (page 85) up to **Notre Dame de la Serra (50min)**. Leave the chapel on the access road, heading due west (there's little traffic, and 10 minutes down you pass some fascinating rocks — like the 'skull' shown on page 85). When the road forks, keep right and come to the main D81b (Porto road; **1h10min**).

Turn left here and, almost immediately, turn right on the track to the lighthouse on **la Revellata**. Soon you can take any of the paths or tracks down to the little cove below to the right (green signs, with the welcome word 'BAR', point the way). When you arrive at the beach (**Plage de l'Alga; 1h30min**), indulge in a swim and some refreshment (although the bar may not be open outside high season).

Take the clear footpath from here all the way along the coast back to Calvi. The path ends at a road junction with the entrance to the Résidences L'Oasis, on the left. Turn right here. The road becomes tarred, passes below some wooden holiday bungalows on the right in about five minutes, then leads to the coastal Calvi/Porto road (D81b) by the entrance to the Résidences Tramariccia. Turn left on the main road and follow it past the CITADEL, back to the RAILWAY STATION in **Calvi (2h10min)**.

## 17 CAPU DI A VETA

**Distance/time:** 14km/8.7mi; 5h10min

**Grade:** Strenuous, with an ascent of 700m/2300ft. Only suitable on fine days *(very dangerous in wet weather or with poor visibility)*. You must be sure-footed, with a head for heights. Inexperienced walkers should *ascend* on the descent route via Pietramaggio (see map): take the road at the roundabout just east of the Casino supermarket, following signs for the 'Hotel Corsica'. From that hotel, keep right, to where the road forks. Turn left on a lane here for just over 200m/yds, then take the orange- and red-waymarked path to the left (signposted).

**Equipment:** as page 50; walking boots, sunhat, warm clothing and plenty of water recommended; *IGN map 4149 OT*

**Access:** 🚌 to/from Calvi; 🚗 travelling by car, you can begin and end the walk at Notre Dame de la Serra; see footnote page 86.

**Short walk/picnic suggestion: Notre Dame de la Serra** (5km/3mi; 1h35min; fairly easy ascent/descent of 200m/650ft). Follow the main

*Views of Notre Dame de la Serra, including the Capu di a Veta (left).
This skull-like rock (bottom right) is on the motor road to the chapel.*

walk to the chapel above Calvi. Notre Dame de la Serra is an ideal place
for an evening picnic, when the sun bathes Calvi's citadel in a golden
glow (photograph page 27). Picnic on the balcony by the chapel or climb
the hillock on the west side of the chapel. Then return the same way.

From start to finish, you have sweeping views over the
Calvi Gulf. Scaling great swellings of hillside rock, and
pushing your way through perfumed maquis, you reach
the summit of the Capu di a Veta (703m/2305ft). From
here you have a magnificent view over the gulf and the
amphitheatre of hills behind it.

**The walk starts** at the RAILWAY STATION in **Calvi**: walk
up steps to the main street (Avenue de la République),
cross it, and turn left. Now take the first turn to the right
(just past the youth hostel). Then take the first left (signpost
'STADE'). Turn right in front of the stadium, pass the
'ANTENNE MEDICALE' (small hospital) on the right, then go
left towards 'LES ALOES'. When the road forks 400m/yds
further on, keep left on the road indicated as a cul-de-sac
(sign: 'EDF'). Pass a turn to the right and, when your road
curls up to the right, watch out for a small sign 'NOTRE
DAME DE LA SERRA' at the right of the entrance to VILLA DE
IRIS on your left (**15min**). This sign directs you along a short
passage leading to a climb over smooth rock with some
steps. You rise to a field, where you can see the chapel,
Notre-Dame de la Serra, ahead. Take the clear, maquis-
lined footpath just to the right of the field. Orange and red
waymarks take you all the way to the chapel, **Notre Dame
de la Serra (50min)**.

Leave the chapel the way you entered it, and head left
along the main track, towards the Capu di a Veta. At the

fork 100m/yds along, bear right. Adorned with a cross, the peak fills in the picture ahead. At the next fork, eight minutes later, go left. Another fork follows within 15 minutes; bear right (the way to the left is an optional return). When the main track ends (**1h35min**), continue on a rough lane, swinging back to the left and climbing steeply. The lane fizzles out at a pass overlooking a severe, rocky valley. Continue on the path opposite the nearby POWER PYLON. Head straight up, ignoring a path off left.

You climb through a narrow passage in the ridge; small cairns and orange and red dots mark the way. Once through the gap, you descend briefly. Scrambling round the rocky hillside, you edge along a ledge, where the going is a bit vertiginous. *Watch for the waymarks and go carefully on the loose stones.* Just over 15 minutes off the track, you come out to a cleavage in the ridge and have views on both sides: Calvi and the gulf to the left and the unspoilt turquoise Nichiareto Bay to your right. Eight minutes later your views expand to encompass the enclosing arm of the Calvi Gulf — the Punta Spano. Lumio (Walk 18) is on the hills across the bay.

Ascending, remain on the left side of Veta's inclines until you reach the SUMMIT, the **Capu di a Veta** (**2h45min**). Here you can sit back and take in this aerial view over the gulfs and surrounding hills. Mount Cinto, the island's highest point, is the shark's fin-shaped peak that rises out of the backbone of mountains. The Figarella and Fiume Seccu river plains form a vast fan around the bay.

Descending, take an easier route. Heading in the direction of Mount Cinto, find the orange waymarks of your continuation (southeast, roughly 140°). Facing Calvi, descend the right-hand flank of the peak. You drop quickly, through a mass of vegetation. The path appears to come out at the end of a road, but in fact turns sharply right, descending into the bed of the **Ruisseau de Vivariu** (**4h**), where you cross the stream and bear left. Keep your eye open for a few twists and turns in the path for the next 10 minutes, until you reach a road. Turn right downhill, cross a small stream, and go right at a junction.* Turn left at the junction by the Hotel Corsica on the outskirts of **Pietramaggio**. The main N197 is straight ahead, and the RAILWAY STATION lies just under 2km to the left (**5h10min**).

---

*If you go straight ahead here, after 130m/yds a red-waymarked path on the left (currently signposted 'Boucle des Autriciens') rises 175m/575ft through maquis back to your outgoing track, from where you could return to Notre Dame de la Serra, if you began the walk there.

# 18 CATERI • OCCI • LUMIO

**See also photograph page 31**

**Distance/time:** 8km/5mi; 2h15min

**Grade:** easy ascent (160m/525ft) and descent (200m/650ft); good tracks and paths throughout; *sparse* orange waymarking after the 1h-point.

**Equipment:** as page 50; take a sunhat!; *IGN maps 4149 OT, 4249 OT*

**Access:** 🚐 taxi or with friends to the Couvent de Marcasso, near Cateri; taxi back from Lumio (or 🚌 from Ondari, 4.5km southeast of Lumio on the N197; Timetable 12)

**Alternative walk: Occi circuit** (6km/3.7mi; 1h50min; moderate ascent/descent of 255m/835ft; *sparse* orange waymarking). 🚐 to the north entrance to Lumio on the N197; park just inside the road, opposite the Hotel Chez Charles. Take the lane behind Chez Charles (sign: 'Village d'Occi'). This becomes a track, then a stone-laid mule trail which rises to the ruined village of Occi (40min). From Occi follow a path which ascends southeast, then descends to a crossing trail (1h05min). Turn left to the little chapel of Notre Dame de la Stella, then retrace your steps to this junction and keep straight on (due west), to descend quite steeply to Lumio.

**Picnic suggestion: Occi** (3km/1.9mi; 1h10min; easy ascent/descent of 165m/540ft). Follow the *Alternative* walk to Occi; return the same way.

D iscover the enchanting villages of the Balagne on foot. For a change you don't have to climb hundreds of metres for an unforgettable view; wonderful rural vistas accompany you all along these hills. See also Walk 19.

**Start the walk** facing the front door of the **Couvent de Marcasso**: descend the mule trail at the right of the garage. Heading above fields and beside tired stone walls, you arrive at **Lavatoggio (15min)**. Walk up to the D71 and turn right. After about 60m/yds, climb steps on the left (faded orange waymark). At the top, turn right on the ALLÉE ROGER

*Approaching the chapel of Notre Dame de la Stella (at the right in the photograph), with Capu Bracajo rising behind it. Fields of grain, hedgerows, and old stone walls and buildings characterise this walk, which is best done late in the day if you want good colour in the valleys and on the Balagne villages.*

*The village of Occi was probably founded in the 15th century by people living on the coast in uncertain times, who moved inland to flee pirate raids. By the late 1800s there were only 60 inhabitants left, and when the last died in the early 1900s, the village was abandoned. Just a couple of years ago, the church in the foreground was completely restored (partly financed by Laetitia Casta, a French model and actress who comes from Lumio). Services are now held at the church once a year, at Pentecost. The local people do not want the village to become commercialised, so it is only accessible on foot.*

DASSONVILLE (sign on the right: 'LUMIO 1H25MIN'). You look back across the valley to the square church tower at Aregno and to Sant' Antonino straddling a hill (photographs pages 31 and 29). Continue up the lane, then track, to a tiny chapel, **San Giovanni di Venti (30min)**.

Keep on the track straight past this chapel, heading towards Capu Bracajo in the setting shown on page 87, until you come to another little chapel, **Notre Dame de la Stella (1h)**. Keep straight ahead on the track past this chapel, too. But after about 100m/yds go right, uphill. (Straight ahead is the path to Lumio followed at the end of the Alternative walk.) Ignoring any paths to the right, rise past the odd wheat threshing floor, enjoying fine views to Calvi, la Revellata, the Bonifatu mountains, and Capu d'Occi up to the right.

Beyond a small pass below Capu d'Occi, the trail descends to the dramatically perched ruins of **Occi (1h35min)**. From the church, with the BUILDING DATED

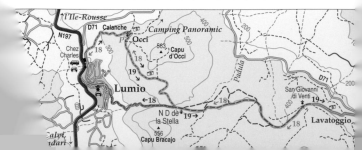

1785 on your left, walk towards a stone wall and then left, away from Occi, to a path that leads straight towards Calvi and the lighthouse on La Revellata. (Ignore a good path on the right; it goes down to Camping Panoramic on the D71.)

You descend an old stone-laid mule trail (some orange waymarks), soon zigzagging down through pink boulders (the 'Calanche'). At a three-way fork, take either track to the right. Coming onto a lane, follow it behind the Hotel Chez Charles, then fork left uphill into **Lumio (2h15min)**.

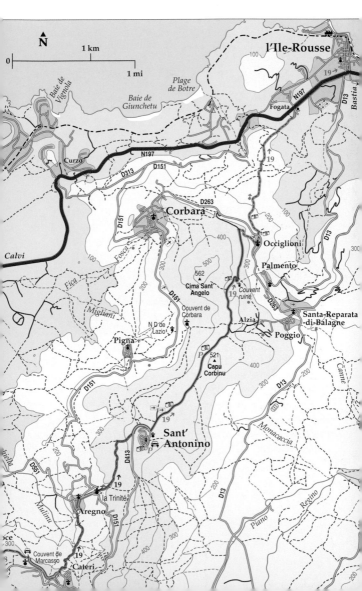

# 19 FROM SANT' ANTONINO TO L'ILE-ROUSSE

**See map pages 88-89; see also photographs on pages 29 and 31**

**Distance/time:** 9km/5.6mi; 2h10min

**Grade:** easy descent of 450m/1475ft on good tracks and paths. The way-marks are faint and infrequent, but the route is straightforward.

**Equipment:** as page 50; wear a sunhat!; *IGN maps 4149 OT, 4249 OT*

**Access:** 🚖 taxi or with friends to Sant' Antonino; return by 🚌 from l'Ile-Rousse (Timetable 12)

**Alternative walk: la Balagne** (21km/13mi; 6h; moderate, but long; overall ascent: 550m/1800ft; descent 650m/2130ft; *little shade*). Access: 🚖 taxi to Chez Charles in Lumio; return as main walk. Follow *Alternative walk 18* to the chapel of Notre Dame de la Stella. Then use the map and *carefully* follow waymarking/signposting, remembering that you should always be on a *good* path (the remains of an old mule trail). On the stretch from Lavatoggio to the Couvent de Marcasso, be sure not to drop down too far; the footpath is only 25m/80ft below the road. Turn left at the cemetery just before Cateri: the trail continues from below the Hotel San Dume. Go through Aregno to the Pisan Romanesque Eglise de la Trinité (12C), then climb to Sant' Antonino and pick up the walk below.

**Picnic suggestions: Sant' Antonino** (easy, 10-15min on foot, *but no shade*; best suited to an *evening* picnic). Walk up to the hilltop in the middle of Sant' Antonino (view to Algajola Bay, the inland mountains, and over Sant' Antonino itself), or follow the main walk to the view over Corbara.

Together with Walk 18, this short downhill ramble gives you a good overview of the Balagne. But if the weather is cool and breezy, then I heartily recommend the *Alternative* walk above — it's a 'grand tour' in every sense!

**Start the walk** in **Sant' Antonino**, at the village CAR PARK. Take the dirt track 100m/yds to the left of the CHURCH, heading for a CEMETERY on a rise. At a fork about 200m/yds along, go right (left *may* be signposted to the Couvent de Corbara). This sandy track is *not* signposted, but it affords better views and avoids an unnecessary climb in full sun from Corbara. You rise over a PASS and pass a track up to the relay station on **Capu Corbinu** (**15min**). This is a brilliant viewpoint down over Pigna and Corbara, with the Couvent de Corbara in the foreground, backed by the Cima Sant' Angelo — a lovely picnic spot.

At a T-junction (**25min**), keep left downhill. Two minutes later you come to a barrage of signposts on the left, some of them broken. The path from the Couvent de Corbara comes in here from the left. Keep right here (you may spot the occasional orange flash). As you pass below the **Cima Sant' Angelo**, you have a good view down to l'Ile-Rousse and its lighthouse; in the middle distance, cypresses and a slender church tower announce Occiglioni, the next village en route.

You soon pass a beautiful old ruined convent on the right (**40min**). Palmento is the village just below to the east. Be sure to take a break under the venerable oak here — the only shade for miles around! Then follow the track into an S-bend. You'll be surprised when you see that you have *passed* Occiglioni's church! Don't worry, your turn-off back to the village is just ahead: just opposite a sign on the left pointing back the way you came, take the old mule trail down to the right (**50min**). Dark red flashes guide you down past the village CEMETERY and WASH-HOUSE (both on the left), into **Occiglioni** (**55min**). Walk to the left of the CHURCH on a beautifully cobbled path and then follow the cobbles downhill under an arch. Go straight ahead between the houses and in two minutes you come to the main D263, by a viewpoint with an iron cross.

Go down the concrete steps just to the left of the viewpoint (signpost: 'ILE ROUSSE'). At a Y-fork immediately, keep left. From up here you enjoy good views of your final destination. You pass a lovely old FOUNTAIN on the left (**1h10min**); cobbles underfoot remind you that this was once a beautiful old mule trail; sadly, it is now mostly sand or rubble. Seven or eight minutes later, a stream merges with the path, and the going may be a bit wet. You've lost the views of l'Ile-Rousse by now. At a fork, go straight ahead (**1h22min**). The sign here says that l'Ile-Rousse is just 15 minutes away — but the station is still *50 minutes* away. Continue through the heavily aromatic maquis. Cross over a track to a house on the left and rejoin the path. Two minutes later, go straight across a sandy cross-path. Ten minutes later, at a complicated inter-section, just go straight ahead on bedrock. Six minutes later pass a house on the left with a very pretty fountain. On reaching a tarred lane two minutes later, turn left down to the main N197, by a BAR/DISCO (**1h45min**). Turn right to **l'Ile-Rousse**; after enjoying a drink in the plane-shaded square (photograph page 31), walk on to the RAILWAY STATION by the port (**2h10min**).

*View over l'Ile-Rousse*

# 20 PLAGE DE L'OSTRICONI

*These ancient junipers growing in the dunes play an important ecological role, forming a screen behind which maquis and trees can grow.*

**See also photo pages 8-9**     **Distance/time:** 6km/3.7mi; 1h45min

**Grade:** easy after a steep, rough descent; be prepared to wade; *no shade*

**Equipment:** as page 50; sunhat, waders, bathing things, plenty of water; *IGN map 4249 OT*

**Access:** 🚌 to/from the Plage de l'Ostriconi: the road runs north off the N1197 some 2.5km west of the Ile-Rousse/St-Florent junction to a camp site entrance; park a bit further on, in one of the lay-bys.

**Picnic suggestions:** coastal path (no shade), footbridge (shade nearby)

The Plage de l'Ostriconi lies at the western end of the Désert des Agriates and the Sentier du Littoral (see Walk 33). It is one of the few areas of dunes in Corsica and a 'textbook' habitat for plants and birds. Your approach is magnificent; the river meanders through rich farmlands and trees to its mouth at a vivid turquoise sea, collared by a necklace of white sand (see pages 8-9).

**The walk begins** at the PARKING AREA above the beach. Scramble down the steep path, then wade across the mouth of the **Ostriconi River**. Cross the **Plage de l'Ostriconi** and, on the far side, rise up on a track; then fork left on the coastal path. After crossing a streambed, the path runs between two small RUINS (**i Magazini**) and then two old stone pillars (navigational aids). You can end the walk at the **Anse de Vana** (**45min**) with a swim, or follow the ongoing path as far as you like.

On your return take the sandy inland track (arrow carved in stone). You pass a signboard for the SENTIER DU LITTORAL (**1h10min**). A few minutes later, at a Y-fork, turn down right to the beach. Walk along the back of the beach until you come to a juniper- and reed-edged creek. Follow the cart track beside it (be prepared to wade) to a little FOOTBRIDGE over the **Etang de Foce** — an idyllic spot, with eucalyptus and farmland on the far side. Then retrace your steps to the CAR PARK (**1h45min**).

# 21  FROM CALENZANA TO BONIFATU

**Distance/time:** 11km/6.8mi; 4h

**Grade:** moderate, with a overall ascent of some 400m/1300ft

**Equipment:** as page 50; walking boots, warm clothing, bathing things, ample water recommended; *IGN map 4149 OT*

**Access:** 🚐 taxi or with friends to Calenzana (12.5km from Calvi), or 🚐 (Timetable 10; in *high season only);* return with the same taxi from the *auberge* at Bonifatu (or phone 04 95 65 30 36 for a taxi when you arrive).

This hike follows the start of the 'Mare e Monti' ('Sea and Mountains') footpath. In spring the maquis is a tangled bouquet of colour. The Figarella River, alongside which you climb as you near Bonifatu, will probably entice you to spend the rest of the day there with its inviting and invigorating pools.

**Start** in **Calenzana**, an important centre in the Genoese era. With your back to the 17th/18th-century church of **St-Blaise** and its baroque campanile, go up the alley at the right of the BAR/TABAC (the chapel of **Ste-Croix** is on your right). Pass a BOUCHERIE on the right and rise to a higher square with the MAIRIE and a WAR MEMORIAL. Follow the orange (Mare e Monti) and red (GR) waymarking past the POSTE on the left and up into the QUARTIER DE L'EVEQUE (it's worth looking around this area, with its beautiful old wooden doors and bookbinder's *atelier.* Signs and way-marks guide you to the right along a narrow street, then left up to the little **Oratoire St-Antoine de Padue** on the left. The waymarked footpath proper begins here.

When the GR20 eventually forks off left (**1h**), keep right, following orange waymarks. You look out over the flat-bottomed valley of the Fiume Seccu. Once over the pass (**Bocca u Corsu**; 581m/1906ft) you drop down into the vast, tapering Figarella Valley, just where it disappears into the central massif. Not long after the third stream crossing, you come to a TRACK (**1h50min**) and keep straight ahead uphill for 'BONIFATU'. A little over 1km along, past a turn-off to the left, you look up into rocky mountains.

Eventually the valley closes up, and you cross the **Figa-rella** (**3h05min**). Here you leave the track and follow the river, turning left up a wide signposted path. Scramble along the old watercourse, briefly floundering across rocks and boulders and passing some inviting POOLS, the largest of which is just 100m before your turn-off (**3h25min**). It draws you to a halt, and you soon forget the time. Cool off, then bake yourself dry on one of the gigantic boulders! No need to hurry; the walk ends only 35 minutes uphill.

A rough 15-minute ascent brings you onto the Boni-fatu road at **Bocca Reza**; turn left here. After 150m you

*Calenzana: the church of St-Blaise and campanile (left) and the bookbinder's atelier (right). Below: rock pools in the Figarella River.*

pass a path off right (part of the circuit followed in Walk 23). You now look up into a striking valley framed by mountains. High above the treeline, bare and forbidding crags rise abruptly. Far below, green pools sit cradled in the valley floor. Just after passing a FORESTRY HOUSE, you cross a BRIDGE (picnic area with SPRING) and arrive at the **Auberge de la Forêt** at **Bonifatu** (**4h**).

# 22 BONIFATU • REFUGE DE CARROZZU • SPASIMATA BRIDGE • BONIFATU

**Distance/time:** 14km/8.7mi; 5h45min

**Grade:** fairly strenuous, with an ascent of 740m/2430ft lasting two hours. Not suitable in cold or changeable weather. While the descent to the Spasimata bridge might prove unnerving for some, *I heartily recommend this walk to anyone who is fit and sure-footed — even beginners.*

**Equipment:** as page 50; walking boots, warm clothing, bathing things and plenty of water recommended; *IGN map 4149 OT*

**Access:** 🚗 car from Calvi via the airport road and the D251, to/from the *auberge* at Bonifatu (22km); paid parking in season

**Shorter walks/picnic suggestions:** Follow the main walk to the 20min-point (**Ruisseau de Lamitu**) or the 50min-point (**Ruisseau de Meta di Filu**). Good streamside picnicking, in sun or shade. (There is also a shady picnic area, with a spring and stone table just by the bridge at Bonifatu.)

**Y**ou scale the wall of a deep valley in the shade of a forest, with the sound of tumbling water following you all the way. Rock pinnacles tower above you, streams cascade across your path, and two suspension bridges add a touch of excitement.

**The walk begins** at **Bonifatu**. Head up the wide forestry road, with the **Auberge de la Forêt** on your right and the boulder-strewn **Figarella River** below on your left. A thick blanket of trees covers the slopes. The track peters out by a ford (*gué;* **25min**) on the left over the **Ruisseau de Lamitu**, signposted to the 'Refuge d'Ortu di u Piobbu 3h'. Here we go uphill to the right, on a path signposted 'REFUGE CARROZZU 2H' and waymarked with two yellow flashes. Up ahead, the valley forks, and an imposing pyramid of rock splits the ravine. Snow may still linger on the peaks.

A stream is crossed (**Ruisseau de Meta di Filu; 50min**);

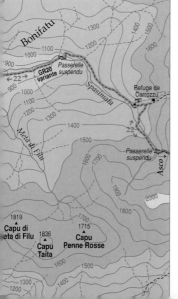

then you cross the **Ruisseau de Spasimata** on a first SUSPENSION BRIDGE (**1h 15min**). Wire ropes act as 'handrails'. On the far side of the river, your ascent becomes more noticeable. Two more stream crossings follow.

You pass the remains of hillside terracing and a stone table and benches beside the stream (**2h**). A small STONE SHELTER lies a couple of minutes further on. Go steeply uphill, to another signposted junction. The refuge is left; Asco and the Spasimata bridge right. First go left. You walk into a picture postcard. Over the hillside birches and pines, you have views of the lush plains far below, framed by the near-vertical valley walls. A sloping hill of smooth rock slides down on your right, and behind it, in complete contrast, a sharp wall of rock cuts across the landscape. A cone-shaped peak looming up across from you dominates the scene. The wonderfully-sited **Refuge de Carrozzu** (**2h30min**) sits just around the bend. For the use of overnight visitors only, it's fully equipped and open all year, but only manned from June to October (when the guardian will usually only sell refreshments to GR20 walkers).

Returning to the junction, follow the GR20 (red and white flashes) towards Asco. You descend towards the valley floor (wire ropes help protect awkward passages). The **Spasimata bridge** spans the river just below you now. A cascade splashes down into the beautiful pool 20m/60ft beneath it. This is a very exhilarating spot. A wire rope helps you down the final drop to the bridge. If crossing the bridge 'gives you the jitters', don't look down through the slats — look up into the distance. Once over the bridge (**2h55min**), you can always wander a bit further on, following the GR20 towards Asco, but the going gets very tough. Picnicking beside the pool here is very popular 'in season'. From every angle the mountain scenery is tremendous.

Return to **Bonifatu** by the same route (**5h45min**).

*This bridge over the Spasimata was replaced by a sturdier model in the late 1990s; nevertheless, only two people should be on it at one time.*

## 23 ERBAGHIOLU CIRCUIT

See map pages 94-95  **Distance/time:** 11km/6.8mi; 5h
**Grade:** strenuous, with an ascent of 760m/2500ft; you must be sure-footed and have a head for heights. The circuit is well waymarked (red).
**Equipment:** as page 50; walking boots, warm clothing and water recommended; *IGN map 4149 OT*
**Access:** 🚗 car from Calvi via the airport road and the D251, to/from the *auberge* at Bonifatu (22km); paid parking in season

Huffing and puffing up to the pine woods and grassy slopes, you look out along the winding Figarella Valley to the Gulf of Calvi, before disappearing back into the forest on your return to Bonifatu.

**Begin** at the **Auberge de la Forêt** at **Bonifatu**. Walk back along the D251 (SPRING on the left just by the bridge) for 10 minutes. Some 150m/yds short of the **Bocca Reza**, take the path heading half-left up the bank (red waymark). You'll be climbing for the next two hours; small streams provide good resting places en route. As you leave the woods, Calvi — just a smudge of white — and the gulf are glimpsed through the hills. Cyclamen, violets, and buttercups lie along the path; moss and grass cushion the hillside. The air is fresh, and the odd fir tree enhances this alpine atmosphere.

Knees-a-quiver, you pass your signposted turn-off back to Bonifatu and a SPRING on the left not far below the **Bocca di Bonassa** (1153m/3780ft; **2h20min**), the highest point on the 'Mare e Monti'. From here a dip in the distant hills reveals the Fango Valley (Walk 24) and some scattered habitations. After taking a break, return to the junction and follow both the red circuit waymarks and orange 'Mare e Monti' flashes to the highest pass on this walk, the **Bocca di l'Erbaghiolu** (1195m/3920ft; **2h55min**).

Then begin the steep zig-zag descent down to the upper reaches of the **Ruisseau de Nocaghia** and follow it all the way down the valley, with the sound of rushing water below through the trees. After crossing this stream (**4h 25min**), continue down to the BRIDGE on the D251 and turn right, back to the **Auberge de la Forêt** at **Bonifatu** (5h).

*At the Bocca di Bonassa*

97

## 24 FROM BONIFATU TO TUARELLI

**Map begins on pages 94-95 and ends below**

**Distance/time:** 19km/11.8mi; 6h15min

**Grade:** strenuous climb of 620m/2035ft at the outset; the rest is a doddle … but long. You must be sure-footed and have a head for heights. Not recommended in changeable weather.

**Equipment:** as page 50; walking boots, sun protection, warm clothing, bathing things and *plenty of water* recommended (the *only* source of water en route is the spring below the Bocca di Bonassa); *IGN map 4149 OT*

*The Fango*

**Access:** 🚗 taxi or with friends to the *auberge* at Bonifatu; return with the same driver from either the Pont de Tuarelli-Chiorna on the D351 south of the Fango River or from the nearby *gîte d'étape* (Auberge l'Alzelli; only open May-September).

**Alternative walk: Bocca di Bonassa** (12km/7.4mi; 4h05min; strenuous, with an ascent of 620m/2035ft. You must be sure footed and have a head for heights. Not recommended in changeable weather. Equipment as for *Walk 23* (page 97). Follow *Walk 23* (map pages 94-95) to the Bocca di Bonassa and return the same way.

**Short walk/picnic suggestion: Fango River** (7km/4.3mi; 2h30min; easy). Stout shoes will suffice, but take a sun protection and swimming things. 🚗 Park on the Fango River road (D351), either at the first bridge (Ponte Vecchiu, 2.5km from the D81, shown overleaf) or the second (Pont de Tuarelli-Chiorna; 5km from the D81). In either case, cross the bridge to the north bank of the Fango, and follow the orange waymarks of the 'Mare e Monti' to the other bridge, then return the same way. From the beautiful arched Ponte Vecchiu the path is signposted 'Tuarelli'; from the second bridge you must first walk left uphill on a lane, to a signpost for 'Galeria', then turn left. (A right turn leads to the Auberge l'Alzelli, a simply idyllic refreshment stop.) There are picnic spots galore on this route, many of them with ample shade. About halfway along in either direction, you come to an exquisite river setting, where pale green-to-blue pools are set deep in a riverbed of rose-coloured, grey, and mauve rock. There's another irresistible swimming spot just beneath the Ponte Vecchiu.

This walk begins its descent where Walk 23 first pauses for breath — at the Bocca di Bonassa. You lose sight of the Figarella Valley, but the landscape opens out to

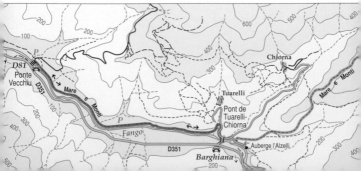

another valley, equally as long, where the magnificent Fango River flows. If you've always preferred the sea to a river for swimming, you might just change your mind! The short walk makes a perfect 'river day', as opposed to a 'beach day', and is ideal for picnicking.

**Begin** by following Walk 23 (page 97) to the **Bocca di Bonassa (2h15min)** — the highest point on the 'Mare e Monti' trail, which you join at this pass. Now follow *orange* waymarks into a very steep zigzagging descent (perhaps on your backside in wet weather). *Watch the waymarking all the way!* A rocky nodule some 200m/ 650ft downhill, on a deep bend, affords a good view down the valley. Near the valley floor you'll encounter oaks again; the forest is more spacious, allowing some of them to grow to a massive girth. Bouldery streambeds (some of them slippery; watch your footing!) lie at regular intervals. Soon the way is again lit up by flowers.

Eventually you cross a refreshing stream, the **Ruisseau de Scala (4h)**, lined by some splendid old chestnuts. Fifteen minutes later pass through a small chestnut grove. Don't be surprised to encounter livestock and even some wild pigs along the path. The waymarking may have vanished by now, but the contouring route is very obvious, and you need not watch out for any turn-off.

The **Bocca di Lucca** (589m/1932ft; **4h50min**) is a good viewpoint towards Galéria's gulf — and all the way back to the Bocca di Bonassa. At the junction here, head left

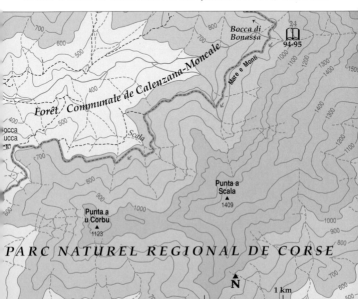

(southeast), over the pass. The next junction comes up at another SADDLE (331m/1085ft; **6h**): keep straight ahead here. Tuarelli soon appears below on the river flat. Old stone walls give it a touch of charm.

Within 15 minutes you meet a lane: turn right, towards the hamlet. Cross the bridge (**Pont de Tuarelli-Chiorna; 6h15min**) to meet your taxi on the D351. Take a look at the crystal-clear pool below this bridge; you may not be able to resist jumping into this Olympic-sized waterhole. But if you've asked the taxi to collect you at the idyllic Auberge l'Alzelli on the north side of the bridge (only open May-September), you can always take a dip there!

*Ponte Vecchiu (Short walk): the Fango River cuts through the valley floor, leaving many lovely green-tinted rock pools along its course.*

## 25 BARGHIANA • BOCCA DI CAPRONALE • BARGHIANA

**Distance/time:** 14km/8.7mi; 7h20min

**Grade:** very strenuous, with a climb of 1000m/3300ft. Cold and dangerous in bad weather. Possibility of vertigo — *and of landslides*. Only recommended for experienced and hardy hikers; *no waymarking*.

**Equipment:** as page 50; walking boots and warm clothing recommended; *IGN map 4149 OT*

**Access:** 🚗 car to/from Barghiana (41.5km from Calvi via the airport route). From the village continue by car on the rough track (D351) just at the left of the church and cemetery. Park at the Ponte di e Rocce (3.5km). If you're not in a 4WD vehicle, check your insurance for tyre damage — although most people do drive here in normal hire cars.

**Short walk/picnic suggestion: Ruisseau de Campottoli Rossi** (5km/3mi; 1h30min; easy ascent of 160m/525ft on a track). Follow the main walk to the 45min-point, where a small footbridge crosses a cascading stream, and return the same way. Picnic by the stream.

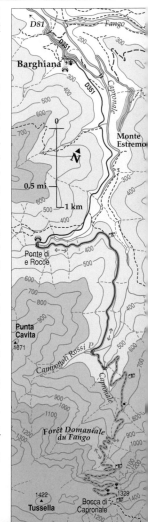

The rewards for this walk will cost you dearly, so save the next day for the beach! This little-frequented footpath climbs through a pleasant evergreen oak forest, following an old mule trail to the Niolo Plateau. Out of the woods, you come to the end of the valley and find that you're completely walled in! Sheer mountains tower above you. But your spectacular onward trail takes you up and over these walls, along precipitous ledges. In all my hiking on Corsica, only on these summits have I spotted the rare moufflon, but I have to confess it's usually only their bums, as they vanish amidst the rock. Good luck!

**The walk begins** above **Barghiana**, at the **Ponte di e Rocce** (limited parking, in shade). Continue along the track, behind the sign 'CIRCULATION INTERDIT'. As the track bends south after 1km, you have a wonderful view towards the towering peaks of the Cinto range. The **Ruisseau de Capronale**, a tributary of the Fango, flows below you. Soon Capu Tafunatu (2335m/ 7660ft) catches your eye. A gaping

101

hole the size of a tennis court pierces the peak. According to one legend, the devil bragged to St Martin that he could build a bridge over the torrents of the Golo in a single night. All was complete bar the keystone, when a shepherd in prayer disturbed a nearby cock, causing it to crow. In a fit of rage, the devil hurled his hammer in the air. It flew straight through Capu Tafunatu, landing just off the west coast and thus forming the Girolata Gulf...

The track narrows to a path and the gushing **Ruisseau de Campottoli Rossi** is crossed on a footbridge (**45min**). *(The Short walk turns back at this delightful spot.)* Continue up the path, after about 30 minutes passing the remains of the old canton house, set back in the trees above the path, just beyond a small bubbly stream. Animal tracks make the route a bit confusing, but there *is* one main mule trail. Pass a SPRING on your left 15 minutes up from the canton house.

The valley terminates in sheer curving walls just up ahead. Crossing the valley floor, you get a view back onto the rose-coloured hills of the Cinto range. And then the *real* climb begins. The path ascends in sweeping zigzags, frequently interrupted by animal paths cutting straight up the sides of the slopes. Stretches of scree will slow you up. It's more than likely, too, that you'll have to squeeze past timid cows and calves grazing the narrow ledges. Please go *very quietly,* and give them 'right of way'.

Finally you reach the PASS (**Bocca di Capronale;** 1329m/4360ft; **3h45min**). The prominent peak to the north is Punta Silvareccia (1964m/6442ft). The path continues round the valley to the Niolo. As lovely as this vista may be, your eyes will always return to those red hills.

From here return the same way, taking the steep gravelly descent slowly. If it's not too late when you get back to the **Ponte di e Rocce** (**7h20min**), how about a dip in one of the Fango's inviting rock pools?

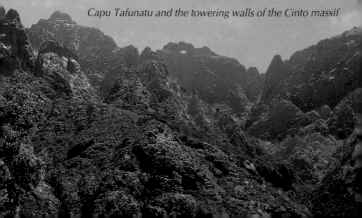

*Capu Tafunatu and the towering walls of the Cinto massif*

# 26 FROM GALERIA TO GIROLATA

**Distance/time:** 13km/8mi; 6h

**Grade:** very strenuous, with an ascent of 784m/2570ft. You must be sure-footed and have a head for heights. Not recommended in changeable weather. Little shade.

**Equipment:** as page 50; walking boots, sun protection, bathing things, *plenty of water* recommended (no springs en route); *IGN map 4150 OT*

**Access:** Unless you are travelling with friends who can take you to Galéria early in the morning and collect you on the D81 late in the afternoon, this walk demands an overnight stay at Girolata (inns, *gîte d'étape:* enquire at the nearest tourist office for information and *book well in advance!*). I suggest taking the 🚢 to Galéria, an overnight stay at Girolata, and returning to Calvi on the same boat the next day. The Christophe Colombe (Timetable 11) is the only boat calling at Galéria and Girolata; all arrangements can be made at their kiosk at the port in Calvi. Otherwise, if you are *very fit* and you *can* arrange for someone to collect you, carry on from Girolata up to the Bocca di a Croce on the D81 (allow 2h and another 300m/1000ft of overall ascent from Girolata).

**Shorter walk: Girolata from the Bocca di a Croce** (10km/6.2mi; 3h-40min; moderate, with overall ascents of about 500m/1640ft). 🚍 to/ from the Bocca di a Croce (on the D81 north of Osani). Stout shoes will suffice, but take ample sun protection and bathing things. *Don't miss this walk!* Try to arrive at Girolata before 11.30 or after 14.00, when the excursion boats are not there. The path begins its descent on the north side of the parking area (with snack bar), by a signpost 'Plage de Tuara 30min; Girolata 1h30min'. The route is a variation of the 'Mare e Monti' trail and is waymarked in orange. You pass a spring on the descent (15min). Near the Plage de Taura, just before a stone wall bordering the path, turn off the 'Mare e Monti' and drop down to the Ruisseau de Tuara and beach (40min). Continue alongside another wall and cross another streambed. As you come back into scrub, you meet the 'Mare e Monti' again, at a junction. Take the inland route here, straight up the ridge. When a path (also 'Mare e Monti') joins you from the right (35min), keep straight on over the ridge and descend to Girolata (25min downhill; 1h40min). Allow 2h for the return, which you can vary by taking the coastal route back to Tuara (see map; orange waymarking).

The invigorating boat journey to Galéria makes this walk unique on Corsica. (It can be a little choppy, so hopefully you have 'sea legs'!) From the port of Calvi superb coastal scenery follows you all the way, from the citadel, via the red cliffs of the Punta Scandola and the maquis-wooded hills that slip off into the sea, to the sheer mountains of granite bursting up out of the Girolata Gulf. Girolata is a beautifully-sited, rustic tourist-trap only accessible by boat or on foot. (You'll see postcards and pictures of it all round the island.) Excursion boats disgorge day-trippers here for a two-hour lunch before returning. However, once the tourists have gone, peace reigns again, and the natural beauty of this tiny fishing port can be really appreciated.

**The walk begins** when the boat has run aground (intentionally) and you have climbed down the ladder and onto

*Girolata*

the beach. Walk up into the characterful old centre of **Galéria**, with the church, *mairie, poste* and a few restaurants (the rest of this beach-orientated village is a touristic hodge-podge). From the west side of the CHURCH, take the narrow road signposted 'HAMEAU DE CALCA' and 'GITE GIROLATA'. The back of the *gendarmerie* will be on your right. When you pass the *gîte* (left), you pick up the first orange flashes of the 'Mare e Monti'. Continue along the road until, about 1 km from the church at Galéria, you see an orange arrow on the road and a sign ('TMM'). This is where your path turns off left. Stone walls flank your route briefly, before it disappears into woods. Fifteen minutes along you encounter two forks, a minute apart: keep right at the first and left at the second, to cross the **Ruisseau de Tavulaghiu**.

Just over the valley floor you rise to a junction. Your way is to the right, and you pass above a muddy RESERVOIR (**1h**) cradled in the valley floor. The cacophony of chorusing frogs is almost deafening. About 15 minutes from the reservoir, you begin a series of stream crossings over the Tavulaghiu (take care on the slippery rocks). Trees draped with vines and creepers shade the way. By now you are steadily ascending up into the high surrounding hills, and despite the zigzags in the path, this stretch is very strenuous. A ROCK 'BALCONY' (**2h15min**) makes a good resting place and viewpoint: you have uninterrupted vistas over the Galéria Gulf and the neighbouring bay. Galéria itself sits back off the shore. The slope is covered in junipers, and in early summer the last of the thorny broom florets add their cheerful colour and delightful fragrance.

Twenty minutes uphill from the viewpoint, you mount the summit of this bumpy ridge and begin to descend along it, accompanied by views to the central massif. Monte Cinto (2706m/8875ft), the island's highest peak, stands head and shoulders above the rest. A brief climb follows, up to a grassy PLATEAU (the **Punta di a Literniccia**; **2h50min**), lightly wooded in holm oaks. Go right at the signposted fork here, remaining on the crest of the ridge. (A left turn leads to the Palmarella Pass on the main road.)

Soon the Girolata Gulf comes into sight far below. This exquisite setting is dramatised by a twin-breasted sheer mountain (Monte Seninu, 619m/2030ft) that rears straight up out of the sea and forms the left arm of the bay. The tiny port of Girolata sits comfortably tucked in cushions of maquis-clad hills. Beyond the arm of the bay lies the Porto Gulf and more mountains rising from the sea.

Red-tiled rooftops reveal Girolata. The ridge is crowned by a large Genoese watchtower. Clambering along the crest becomes rather awkward and slow-going. Watch your footing; it's very rocky, and the cliffs drop away quite steeply in places. You go from waymark to waymark, weaving in and out of thorny broom. More wonderful seascapes follow, this time to your right.

The highest point in the climb is reached just below an antenna (784m/2570ft; **4h**). Roughly 15 minutes below the antenna, the path swings back on itself: the main path appears to go left here, but in fact loops back sharply to the right to cross to the north side of the crest yet again. At the **Bocca di Fuata** (**4h30min**) you pass through a clearing and go by the remains of a stone building with a nearby wheat-threshing floor. From here the path descends south along a side-ridge, to the left of the **Capu Licchia**. The turquoise Girolata Gulf becomes brighter as you descend. Heading down the crest, you meet a fork (**5h15min**). Bear right here and cross over the crest, to descend into a small valley. Leaving this valley, you look across the bay to majestic Mount Seninu. The jagged pink and mauve headland of the Punta Scandola, on your right, holds your attention with its rich colouring.

Coming into **Girolata** (**6h**), you step down through a small cluster of modest pink stone dwellings. The prominent remains of the tower dominate the cove. A few wooden sheds, a lean-to restaurant/bar, and even a stable sit in the shade of scruffy eucalyptus trees around the cove, enhancing the 'out-in-the-sticks' appeal of this hamlet. The wooden jetties and handful of yachts hint at tourism, but all is quiet before 11.30 or after 14.00. If you enjoy lobster, this is the place to tuck in; Girolata's *other* income derives from lobster-fishing.

If you're continuing from here on foot — the same day or the next — pick up your continuation at the other end of the beach (signpost: BOCCA DI A CROCE). You can take either strand of the 'Mare e Monti' as far as the Plage de Tuara, where they rejoin to climb to the **Bocca di a Croce**. Allow about 2h — or 2h15min for the inland route.

# 27 CAPANDULA CIRCUIT

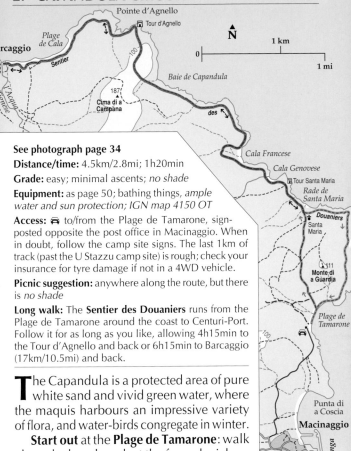

**See photograph page 34**

**Distance/time:** 4.5km/2.8mi; 1h20min

**Grade:** easy; minimal ascents; *no shade*

**Equipment:** as page 50; bathing things, *ample water and sun protection; IGN map 4150 OT*

**Access:** 🚌 to/from the Plage de Tamarone, sign-posted opposite the post office in Macinaggio. When in doubt, follow the camp site signs. The last 1km of track (past the U Stazzu camp site) is rough; check your insurance for tyre damage if not in a 4WD vehicle.

**Picnic suggestion:** anywhere along the route, but there is *no shade*

**Long walk:** The **Sentier des Douaniers** runs from the Plage de Tamarone around the coast to Centuri-Port. Follow it for as long as you like, allowing 4h15min to the Tour d'Agnello and back or 6h15min to Barcaggio (17km/10.5mi) and back.

The Capandula is a protected area of pure white sand and vivid green water, where the maquis harbours an impressive variety of flora, and water-birds congregate in winter.

**Start out** at the **Plage de Tamarone**: walk along the beach and, at the far end, pick up a path heading inland through golden hay-fields (the path to the right is your return route). You cross the low maquis-clothed hills shown on page 34. The tiny **Chapelle Santa Maria** (**30min**) was founded in the 11th century and restored in the 1700s. Not much further on are the intriguing slate-green remains of the grand Genoese **Tour Santa Maria**. It appears to have been sliced down the centre and sits off the shore on a partially-submerged rock. Another watch-tower adorns the largest of the Finocchiarola Islands just to the southeast. Just a short way further along the track, you'll find a lovely sandy cove, ideal for swimming.

Returning, fork left just before the chapel on the **Sentier des Douaniers** (Customs Officers' Path; waymarked), to circle back to the **Plage de Tamarone** (**1h20min**).

See also photograph page 110

**Distance/time:** 5km/3mi; 2h

**Grade:** fairly strenuous, but short, climb of 277m/910ft on good paths (orange waymarking)

**Equipment:** as page 50; IGN maps 4347 OT, 4348 OT

**Access:** 🚌 or 🚐 to/from Lavasina (Timetable 14) on the D80, south of Erbalunga

*Photograph: Convento di Capoccini, Pozzo*

**P**oretto and Pozzo are two enchanting villages, surrounded by a tangle of olive and oak trees. If you don't mind a short, stiff climb, this walk is a gem. At the top you can relax with a drink in Pozzo's square and enjoy the 'balcony' view, before returning to the coast.

**Begin the walk** in **Lavasina**. Head straight up the lane at the left of the 17th-century CHURCH (**Notre-Dame-des-Grâces**). Continue on a path until you can take the right-hand driveway straight ahead. Cross the D54, go straight ahead on a mule track, then turn right at the T-junction.

Soon you're in **Poretto**, on a driveway. Some 35m/yds uphill, bear right along a lane and, within a minute, turn up the steps on your left. Cross a lane and take the first right-hand turn between the houses. Beyond the CHURCH, when the lane swings right, leave it to continue on a path. Pass steps climbing to the left and then an impressive FOUNTAIN. When you reach the D54 again, turn right downhill. After 80m/yds, fork left up a concrete lane. When it ends, pass a garage on your left (dog alert!) and follow an uphill path between high stone walls.

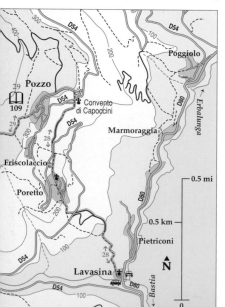

You come out beside the CHURCH shown above. Continue along the alley towards the door of the adjacent **Convento di Capoccini**, but climb steps on the left just before reaching it. Cross the D54 and follow a mule trail to the village road, then turn left to the square in **Pozzo** (**1h10min**).

Return the same way to **Lavasina** (**2h**).

# 29 MONTE STELLO

**See also photograph opposite**   **Distance/time:** 13km/8mi; 7h

**Grade:** strenuous, with an ascent of 1030m/3380ft. Recommended for experienced mountain walkers *only;* don't attempt in changeable weather conditions.

**Equipment:** see page 50; walking boots, warm clothing, ample sun protection and plenty of water recommended; *IGN map 4347 OT*

**Access:** 🚌 to/from Pozzo, reached via the D54 from either Erbalunga or Lavasina. Or on foot from Lavasina (see Walk 28 opposite).

Monte Stello (1307m/4290ft), long thought to be the highest peak on Cap Corse, is in fact 15m/50ft lower than nearby Cima di e Folicce. Nevertheless, it offers superb views out over the cape. There *is* one catch. Monte Stello is not very generous in sharing this panorama; it's inclined to stay hidden by the mists that so often envelop these summits. The spine of the cape is a bleak and unfriendly landscape so, since you're climbing for the view from the top, make sure it's a glorious day!

**The walk begins** in the village square in **Pozzo:** follow the sign 'MONTE STELLU 4H', stepping up between houses. Orange flashes mark the route through the village. The houses and paved alleyways are exceptionally neat. Skirting the back of Pozzo, you come onto your path and head straight on above gardens and out onto hillsides overgrown with maquis. If you have seen the 'Attention — feu' signs everywhere, you'll not be surprised to see blackened trees and shrubs covering the slopes. Your first landmark is a DERELICT STONE COTTAGE (**20min**). Go through a stone wall just beyond it and, eight minutes further up, pass below the remains of another stone building.

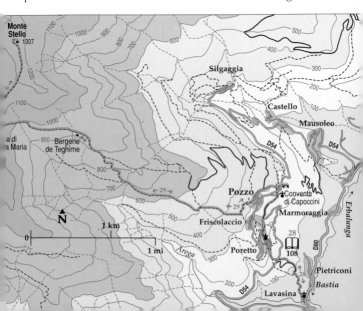

*Pozzo: the old wash-house*

The trail rises gradually to the west, eventually on the north slopes of the **Ruisseau d'Arega**. You climb past a delicious SPRING (it lies just beyond a water tank), to reach the **Bergerie de Teghime (2h15min)**, sheltering against an outcrop of rock. This is a pleasant spot to get your breath back and quench your thirst before the final assault. From here on, a sharp eye is needed to follow the cairns and orange waymarking, both of which may be obscured by the maquis. Your continuation heads off between the two fenced-off enclosures at the *bergerie*. You ascend to a pass, the **Bocca di Santa Maria (3h20min)**.

Over the pass, you look down to a bowl-shaped valley and the small village of Piazza, well concealed from the coast. The arid hills of the Désert des Agriates rise beyond Sant-Florent's shimmering blue gulf. Then Monte Stello, a sprawling rocky hill rising out of this backbone of schist, appears to the right. A couple of minutes downhill to the right you come to a signposted junction, where a path descends left to Olmeta and Nonza. Keep straight on for the summit, now just over 200m/650ft above.

The trail heads directly towards the peak, then rounds it to make the final approach from the north. On the SUMMIT of **Monte Stello (4h)** you'll find an aerial, a hut, the few remains of a small tourist plane that crashed here some years ago … and a fantastic viewpoint over Cap Corse. Bare rocky hills topple off this wavy mountain range, rolling into the sea on either side of you. On the clearest days your view stretches to the many of the island's other summits. To the east and not far below lie the scattered villages of Sisco (swallowed up in greenery) and (further along the coast) Marine de Pietracorbara.

After returning the same way, end the day by popping in to the friendly café in **Pozzo's** SQUARE (**7h**).

*The summit of Monte Stello is a superb lookout point … until the mists come down!*

# 30 CORTE • GORGES DU TAVIGNANO • REFUGE DE LA SEGA • CORTE

**Distance/time:** 32km/20mi; 9h15min

**Grade:** strenuous and long, with a total ascent of about 800m/2300ft, *much of it in full sun.* You must be sure-footed and have a head for heights. It can be very cold and wet; don't attempt in uncertain weather.

**Equipment:** as page 50; walking boots, sun protection, warm clothing, bathing things, *ample food and water* recommended; IGN map 4250 OT

**Access:** 🚌 to/from the 'Mare a Mare Nord' signpost, where the walk begins (see 🚌→ on the map). From the centre of Corte, head south on the main street (towards Ajaccio), passing the citadel on your right. Just before the bridge over the Tavignano, turn right and follow the Chemin de Baliri, below the citadel, to the waymarked path (parking further round to the right). Or 🚂 to Corte (Timetable 21); return on the same train (adds 5km/1h15min to the total walking times).

**Shorter walk: Gorges du Tavignano** (19km/11.8mi; 5h; moderate, with an ascent of 365m/1195ft). Access and equipment as main walk. Follow the main walk to the bridge over the Tavignano (2h45min) and return the same way. *An ideal day out and highly recommended!*

**Alternative, two-day walk: Corte — Refuge de la Sega — Bocca a l'Arinella — Refuge Melo — Funtana d'Argento — Corte** (41km/25.5mi; 12h30min; very strenuous and very long, with a total ascent of about 1300m/4265ft). Only suitable for fit and experienced hikers. It can be very cold and wet; don't attempt in uncertain weather. Plan for an overnight stay at the (recently refurbished/expanded) Refuge de la Sega. There is a guardian from June to October, and food is available, but cooking facilities are also provided. To make a booking, telephone 06 10 71 77 26 (both B&B and half-board offered).

Follow the main walk to the Refuge de la Sega. The next day, continue north on the Mare a Mare Nord, still following orange waymarks. You pass below a bare granite hillside, cross a stream, and rise past a lovely waterfall, through a profusion of lily-like sea daffodils *(Pancratium maritimum)*. Some 350m/1150ft above the refuge you pass alongside the **Bergerie de Boniacce (1h05min)**, a shepherds' outpost with a SPRING at the left of the buildings. Bear left on the track just above the *bergerie*, and rejoin your path some 80m/yds uphill, on the right. Cross another track ten minutes later. In another ten minutes you reach the **Bocca a l'Arinella (1h25min)**: just over this pass, an unsurpassed sight greets you — a sweeping view over the immense Golo Valley and across the 'kingdom' of the Niolo, an isolated and very traditional region of Corsica. This is the turning back point for the hike; home is all downhill!

Return to the last track you crossed and follow it to the left. Ignore a rough track to the right and, later, an orange-waymarked path signposted to Corte forking left (it is easier to stay on the track). You pass the **Refuge Melo (2h15min)**. Some 1h10min along the track (**2h55min**), *watch for your turn-off:* fork left where the track makes a *very sharp bend to the right* (by a small construction, perhaps a sealed reservoir). Now a narrow waymarked path leads you into a magnificent forest of towering Corsican pines, the **Forêt Domaniale du Tavignano.** In a few minutes you cross two small streams; then keep right, round the hillside. Ignore a fork off left within 10 minutes. Some 30 minutes later, just beyond a forestry house, you will be back on the track. If your bottles need refilling, head *right* here for a couple of minutes, to the **Funtana d'Argento**; otherwise go *left* for a few metres/yards, to pick up the continuing path on your right; *take care:* it's rough, steep and overgrown. You rejoin your outgoing route at the SUSPENSION BRIDGE (**5h15min**); head straight back to **Corte**, 2h15min away (**7h30min**, or **12h30min** overall).

I n summer, the most memorable feature of this walk is the lake-sized pool that sits behind the Refuge de la Sega. Tearing yourself away from it is almost impossible; all the day-trippers make a mad dash to catch the last train. Before you reach the refuge, you wind up a gorge, dwarfed by lofty rock walls. Below you lie other tantalisingly beautiful pools.

By car or on foot*, approach the starting point for the walk along the CHEMIN DE BALIRI; it follows the Tavignano. The old citadel crowns the hilltop above on your right in a precarious fashion. As the road completes the circuit of the citadel by bending right, turn left on a short access road to an apartment block (you'll see the orange flashes of the 'Mare a Mare Nord' here). Some 55m/yds along, **begin the walk**: fork left on a path signposted 'VALLÉE DU TAVIGNANU').

Five minutes later, be careful to follow the orange marks up to the right. Soon the old mule trail is circling some hillside terracing. At a fork about 1.5km uphill, follow the orange waymarks to the right. (The left-hand path drops down to some splendid swimming spots if you follow the riverbed for a little over 30 minutes. It is possible to scramble steeply back up to the main path further on.)

The riverbed is a string of beryl-green pools. The valley narrows, and the landscape becomes more dramatic, with rocky salients piercing the pine-studded walls. Landmarks are few but, when you pass a stone hut with a corrugated iron roof in the **Antia Valley**, you're more than halfway to the bridge (Shorter walk). Emerging from this valley, you come to a prominent rocky belvedere and, some 50 minutes later, you cross the **Tavignano** on a STURDY BRIDGE with wooden railings (**2h45min**). *(The Shorter walk turns back at this scenic spot.)*

*If you start at the railway station, head left and make for the town centre, crossing the Restonica and Tavignano rivers. Immediately beyond the Tavignano turn left up the Chemin de Baliri, then see the notes above.

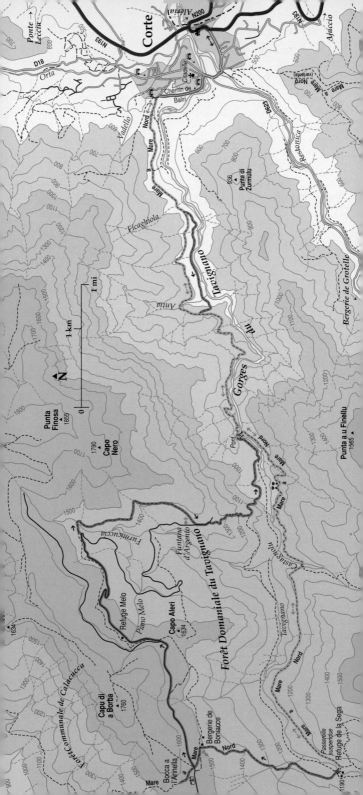

Over the bridge your continuation veers slightly left at first, before turning right above the river. A tough ascent follows. Looking through the trees onto bare rocky summits, you'll notice a thin veil of green lichen covering these heights. The impressive dome of the Capu Aleri (1634m/5360ft) stands out at the right of the valley. Under an hour above the suspension bridge you encounter a 15-minute stretch of path which is quite precipitous; take special care here if it's wet underfoot. After crossing the **Ruisseau de Castagnolu**, ignore the fork to the left.

Beyond a tiny reservoir in the river below, the way mostly contours, and the valley floor is wider. Passing through moss- and lichen-covered rock, you come upon the **Refuge de la Sega** (**5h**) and the pool shown on page 112, an exquisite beauty spot.

Moving on, the same day or the next, the main walk returns to **Corte** along the same route (**9h15min**).

*Walks 31 and 32: Capu a Chiostru, from the Pont de Grotelle*

# 31 LAC DE MELO AND LAC DE CAPITELLO

**See also photograph opposite    Distance/time:** 7km/4.3mi; 4h30min
**Grade:** strenuous, but short, with a steep ascent/descent of 560m/
1835ft. Dangerous if wet. It can be very cold; don't attempt in unpredictable weather. There are *two routes* up to the lakes (see text below).
**Equipment:** as page 50; walking boots, sun protection, warm clothing
and bathing things recommended; *IGN map 4251 OT*
**Access:** 🚐 car to/from the Bergeries de Grotelle at the top of the Restonica road (D623), 15km from Corte. This paying car park is always
busy, so arrive early — or you may have to park well downhill.
**Shorter walk/picnic suggestions: Lac de Melo** (4km/2.5mi; 2h15min;
fairly strenuous ascent/descent of 340m/1120ft). Follow the main walk
to the first lake and picnic there. Or picnic just 30 minutes up the path,
at the grassy area by the Restonica (1h return).

W hether you are a walker or not, do make the effort
to see the Lac de Melo. It's picture-postcard
perfect. The whole Restonica Valley is a wealth of superb
scenery, with overpowering peaks, cascading streams,
and spell-binding glacial lakes. The aching muscles may
not be so memorable, but your photographs surely will.

**The walk begins** at the **Bergeries de Grotelle** (car park,
drinks and cheese for sale). Follow the signpost 'MELO/
CAPITELLO'; yellow paint marks the route. At the outset,
you look straight up at the Capu a Chiostru ridge on your
right (see opposite). The Rotondo massif rises to the left.
Stands of bright green alders illuminate the rocky inclines.
Thorny broom and foxgloves keep you company, as does
the thunder of streams crashing down the mountainsides.

Ten minutes after crossing two streams in quick succession, you reach a fork marked by a large cairn (**30min**).
From here there are *two* routes up to the Lac de Melo. It's
a somewhat easier ascent to take the path to the *left* here
(yellow flashes, cairns). This immediately crosses a grassy
area (a fine picnic spot) and then the **Restonica**. In spring,
however, the river may be too full to cross.

The more adventurous main route keeps to the right of
the Restonica and heads up over bare rock. Not long
before mounting the saddle, you can either haul yourself
up with CHAINS or use the sturdy METAL LADDERS (**55min**).
You eventually cross a pass and find yourself in an amphitheatre of rock. A few steps further on you're at the **Lac
de Melo** (**1h15min**), a dark green mirror filling the basin
floor. Across the lake lies the perfect picnic spot, a grassy
slope shaded by alders. *(The Shorter walk ends here.)*

The Lac du Capitello lies just above the cascading
stream you can see on the right-hand side of the mountain
walls. Relocate the yellow paint (by the tiny stone shelter
for the forestry administration) and climb straight up the

*View from the Lac du Capitello down onto the Lac de Melo (top); there is usually livestock on the Restonica Valley road, so drive carefully!*

steep mountainside. Remain on the right-hand side of the stream for the first 30 minutes. Crossing the stream is a little tricky, and an 'all-fours' climb follows. Red in the face, you  squeeze through a gap in the hillside to find the **Lac du Capitello** (**2h30min**), an indigo-blue pool ensconced in a 40m/130ft-deep hollow. The Capu a i Sorbi (2267m/7435ft) flanks it on the right. You can sit here for hours getting drunk on the intoxicating scenery.

Returning, you can take the other route: cross the **Restonica** at the Lac de Melo and descend beside the right-hand wall of the valley. Then go left at the fork just before the stream and cross the **Restonica** again, to join the main path and return to the **Bergerie de Grotelle** (**4h30min**).

## 32  GORGES DE LA RESTONICA

**See also photograph on page 114**

**Distance/time:** 11km/6.8mi; 4h10min *return*. If you are travelling with friends/a taxi, you can make this a one way walk either down from the Pont de Grotelle (1h45min) or up from the Pont de Frasseta (2h25min).

**Grade:** moderate; descent/reascent of 300m/1000ft. You must be sure-footed (a few rock-falls to cross). Can be very cold; don't attempt in unpredictable weather.

**Equipment:** as page 50; walking boots, warm clothing, bathing things recommended; *IGN map 4251 OT*

**Access:** 🚗 car to/from the Pont de Grotelle on the Restonica road (D623, 15km from Corte). Or, if you prefer to walk *uphill* first, park at the Pont de Frasseta (just by the rock pinnacle shown below; see map).

**Short walk/picnic suggestion:** Touring with friends, you can make this a one-way walk, as under 'Distance' above. Picnic and swim at the river.

I f you've driven up the Restonica road with your heart set on walking up to the lakes (Walk 31), your heart may sink as you reach the Pont de Grotelle! Even out of season, 'flocks' of walkers — like so many sheep — clog the road, all intent on doing the island's best-known hike. You can't help but wonder whether this path above the river itself was opened as an 'overflow' or escape route, for those of us who don't like crowds! But even if you *do* go up to the lakes, then come back to this 'balcony' footpath another day — it's a brilliant hike in a grandiose setting, with many places to picnic by the river or throw yourself into one of its emerald-green rock pools.

**Start out** at the **Pont de Grotelle**, in the magical alpine

*Monte Leonardo's rocky crown, by the Pont de Frasseta*

*Tip:* If you're driving south from Corte and Venaco on the N193, you'll cross the attractive road bridge shown top left before coming to Vivario. On your return — or another day — be sure to take the older road, *below* this bridge, and park by the old road bridge, the Pont du Vecchio (see map pages 66-67). You'll have a better view of the Vecchio River 30m/100ft below you and can look up to one of Gustave Eiffel's lesser-known works of engineering art — this railway bridge rising 100m/330ft above the river. As you can imagine, travelling by train into the interior is simply spectacular!

setting shown on page 114. Cross the bridge, then turn right on a path (signpost: 'PONT DE FRASSETA 1H50MIN'). Ample orange flashes, and some cairns, mark the route all the way to your destination — another bridge a little over 5km downstream. Majestic old pines shade the way

and frame your photographs up to the peaks and down to the rushing **Restonica River**. The path undulates for most of the way, sometimes crossing fairly steep rock-falls (where cairns indicate the route if the orange-painted rocks have slipped away). After bumbling over a side-stream on 'stepping-stone' *boulders,* with a WATERFALL up to left (**35min**), cross straight over a track. Soon the path is just beside the RIVER (**50min**) — a fine place to swim or picnic.

When you come to a wide CROSSING PATH (**1h**), follow it to the left, eventually rising to a tiny grassy PLATEAU (**1h10min**). From here the path zigzags steeply downhill, crosses two adjacent streams, and then runs through ferns bright with foxgloves in spring. On the final short ascent, you look straight out at **Monte Leonardo**, the rocky pinnacle shown on page 117. At the top of the climb (**1h30min**), just opposite this monolith, you come to a sign: 'PONT DE GROTELLE 2H', pointing back the way you came. Turn right at this junction. (The path to the left climbs over to the Tavignano Valley.) Follow the gentle zigzags of the path down to the **Pont de Frasseta** (**1h45min**).

Return to the **Ponte de Grotelle** the same way, allowing 2h10min (**4h10min**).

## 33 SENTIER DU LITTORAL: FROM ST-FLORENT TO PUNTA MORTELLA

**Distance/time:** 19.5km/12mi; 6h20min *from St-Florent;* 13km/8mi; 4h 20min *from the Anse de Fornali*

**Grade:** easy ups and downs on a good coastal path, but virtually *no shade; adequate sun protection is essential.*

**Equipment:** as page 50; stout shoes, ample sun protection, bathing things and *plenty of water* recommended; *IGN map 4348 OT*

**Access:** 🚗 car to/from St-Florent or the Anse de Fornali (saves 2h). By car you can drive along the walking route as far as the 1h-point, avoiding a fairly miserable, dusty track walk. But the tracks are fairly bumpy to *very* bumpy (depending on the year and the season), so *check your insurance for tyre damage liability,* unless you're in a 4WD vehicle.

**Shorter walk/picnic suggestion:** Just follow the main walk for as far as you like and drop down to a cove at any point. The only shade will be from a rocky overhang.

Like Walk 20, this takes in part of the 'Sentier du Littoral', a coastal path stretching the whole length of the Désert des Agriates, from St-Florent to Ostriconi Beach. The land (5000 hectares/12,000 acres) was bought in the 1990s by the Conservatoire du Littoral and is being developed and

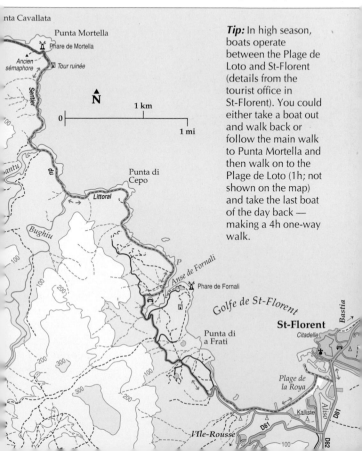

*Tip:* In high season, boats operate between the Plage de Loto and St-Florent (details from the tourist office in St-Florent). You could either take a boat out and walk back or follow the main walk to Punta Mortella and then walk on to the Plage de Loto (1h; not shown on the map) and take the last boat of the day back — making a 4h one-way walk.

managed for the enjoyment of walkers. The whole stretch takes 15 hours, but overnight stops can be made at either Saleccia Beach or Ghignu.

**The walk starts** in the centre of **St-Florent**: follow the main D81 towards L'ILE-ROUSSE. At the port, take the FOOT-BRIDGE to the far side of the **Aliso River** and walk across the sandy **Plage de la Roya** to the end. From the end of the beach head inland; then, almost immediately, turn right up a narrow lane, onto a dirt road. Here you'll find a signpost for the SENTIER DU LITTORAL (**25min**). After a dusty, boring 35 minutes on track, you'll arrive above the **Anse de Fornali** (**1h**), where you'll no doubt spot some cars parked over to the right. Take any path from the parking area down to the coastal path.

Heading west, you pass below some exquisite properties. But your attention will be no doubt be drawn to the wild flowers, the cloud patterns over Cap Corse, and the endless expanse of crystal-clear aquamarine sea. Just walk as far as you like, ending the short walk with a picnic and swim — preferably in a little inlet all your own. Landmarks are the sandy beach at the mouth of the **Fiume Bughiu** (**2h**) and the fiord-like inlet at the **Fiume Santu** (**2h20min**). From here it's another 50 minutes to the **Punta Mortella** (**3h10min**), with its old Genoese WATCHTOWER. (Nelson was so impressed when his fleet attacked this very tower in 1794 that the so-called Martello towers in Kent and Sussex were built and named after this one.) About 100 towers — some round, some square — were built along the coast in the 16th and 17th centuries, mostly as a protection against North African invaders. Their fire-signals could go round the whole island in just two hours!

After perhaps going on to the LIGHTHOUSE, return to **St-Florent** the same way (**6h20min**).

*Anse de Fornali, where the path proper begins*

## 34 MONTE SAN PETRONE

**Distance/time:** 12km/7.5mi; 5h

**Grade:** moderate-strenuous, with an ascent of 780m/2560ft on good tracks and paths, mostly in shade.

**Equipment:** as page 50; walking boots, warm clothing, and *plenty of water* recommended; *IGN map 4150 OT*

**Access:** 🚌 car to/from the Col de Prato, reached via the D71 east from Ponte Leccia, via Morosaglia

**Short walk/picnic suggestion:** San Petru d'Accia (2.5km/1.6mi; 50min; easy; stout shoes will suffice). Follow the main walk to the 17-min point. Turn 90° left here, rising past a water tank on the left. The track reaches the San Petru chapel (half ruined, half new) in 10min — fine picnic spot. The chapel is surrounded by a wall (to keep out the pigs); take the wide downhill path just at the left side of the wall (as you face the chapel) to descend due north, back to the track, then turn right to the Col de Prato.

*Tip:* Just the far side (east) of the Col de Prato, at the Hotel/Restaurant San Petrone, there is a fascinating museum of Corsican artefacts.

On a clear day you can see as far as the Tuscany from the summit of Monte San Petrone, la Castagniccia's 'sacred' mountain. In fact Christianity was brought to the area from the Tuscan islands and, believe it or not, there was a cathedral near the summit in the 12th century!

**The walk begins** at the **Col de Prato**: take the track heading east (large signpost: 'SAN PEDRONE'). Walk to the right of a restaurant/bar and fencing. Twenty paces past the end of the fencing, a path on the left is your return route. Beyond a PIG STYE (**10min**) you come to a three-way fork (**17min**). Take the middle route, almost straight ahead (sign: 'U SAN PETRONE'). *(But for the Short walk, go left.)*

Soon the track is rising gently through beech woods. There are more STYES along this stretch, but the pigs are likely to be running free (*beware:* if you feed them, they'll keep following you and can be very aggressive). Soon a stand of magnificent old chestnut trees interrupts the beech woods. At another fork (**45min**), take the lower track to the right. Ten minutes later, on a RISE IN A SMALL PINE WOOD (**55min**), be sure to leave the track: watch for your signposted path ('SAN PETRONE 1760M') to the left (the main trail heads right to Saliceto). Your path (red paint waymarks) rises to a flat area.

So far the going has been fairly easy, but now the hard work begins. Climbing steading (again through beech), you pass a spring on the right (**Fontana di e Teghie (1h 25min**). Keep left at a fork 150m/yds further on. Eventually you rise to a sunny SADDLE (1536m; **2h05min**) in an alpine setting and enjoy the first long-range views. Ignore the path to the right here; your waymarked path contours left (due north) through old pastures before the final assault.

121

*San Petru d'Accia (top) is sur-rounded by stone walls, to keep out the half-wild pigs Bottom right: at the San Petrone summit*

From the SUMMIT of **Monte San Petrone** (1767m/ 5796ft; **2h 45min**) the long arm of Cap Corse stretches out in the east beyond the green hills of la Castagnic-cia; to the west is la Balagna, backed by the summit of Monte Cinto. And beyond the Tuscan archipelago, even the snow-capped Alps can be seen on a clear day.

Return the same way, but visit the chapel of **San Petru** (see Short walk); from there take the ferny path back to the **Col de Prato** (**5h**).

# 35 FOCE FINOSA AND REFUGE DE PALIRI

See map page 125                    Distance/time: 8km/5mi; 4h

**Grade:** fairly strenuous ups and downs on rocky paths; overall ascent/descent about 560m/1840ft. Don't attempt in changeable weather; dangerous if wet.

**Equipment:** as page 50; walking boots, warm clothing, water recommended; *IGN map 4253 ET*

**Access:** 🚗 car or 🚌 (Timetable 5) to/from the Auberge du Col de Bavella (200m east of the Col de Bavella)

**Short walk/picnic suggestion: Foce Finosa** (5km/3mi; 2h30min; moderate, with an overall ascent/descent of about 310m/1020ft). Follow the main walk for the first 1h15min, then return the same way. There's a lovely grassy picnic place just beyond the 10min-point, in the shade of pines, with fine views of the valley.

The Massif of Bavella, with its towering pink walls of jutting crags and magnificent pine forest, has a magnetic, irresistible beauty. And then there are the views ... some of the finest on Corsica. On these grassy, cushion-soft inclines that hide amidst the rock, no picnic has ever tasted more delicious.

**Start out** at the AUBERGE DU COL DE **Bavella** (200m east downhill from the parking area at the col). Take the forestry track opposite the *auberge,* marked with the red and white flashes of the GR20 and signposted 'PALIRI'. There is a FOUNTAIN here. From the outset you have a superb view that stretches to the sea, but it's the formidable wall of rocky pink crags bulging out of the landscape and blocking your way that holds your attention. Pines wood the sheer slopes. From here the modest settlement of Bavella is concealed by woods. Some 600m/yds along (**10min**), leave the track: fork left on a path (Walk 36 takes the path forking off to the right just before this turning). A steep descent (very slippery when wet) takes you down into a wooded gulley. The inclines are spongy with grass and patched with fern, the pines elegantly tall and straight. This is a lovely picnic setting, with views towards the dramatic, pink-tinted walls of the valley.

The path drops you down onto another track (**40min**), where you turn right. You pass a fork off to the right and soon cross an ebullient stream (**Ruisseau de Volpajola**; you may have to wade across in springtime). Minutes over the ford, a signpost ('REFUGE DE PALIRI') directs you up a path to the right. Zigzag up the steep rocky path to the summits and the **Foce Finosa** (1206m/3960ft; **1h15min**). The Short walk turns back here.

To enjoy the best views from this pass you need to scramble *(with great care)* up onto the crest of the ridge, so that you can see over the pines. The awe-inspiring

The Bavella massif is an unforgettable picnic setting, dominated by
pink-tinted granite cliffs. Above:
view to the Aiguilles de Bavella
from a grassy plateau (the 30min-
point in Walk 36). Left: the Refuge
de Paliri sits just at the foot of the
mighty Punta Tafunata di i Paliri;
there's a table and benches in
front, or a more sheltered spot just
over the ridge to the right.

Aiguilles de Bavella rise inland: massive slabs of rock
lining the valley walls dominate the landscape. On the
coast lies the Gulf of Porto-Vecchio with its scooped-out,
white-collared bays. In your immediate surroundings, the
rock can be anything from a soft pink to a deep rose,
depending on the time of day.

Continuing on to the Refuge de Paliri, descend the very
steep and rocky hill below the pass, looking straight out
to the magnificent Porto-Vecchio Gulf. Fortunately, this
jarring descent changes direction and swings left across
the flank of the ridge, to meet a junction 35 minutes below
the pass. Follow the GR20 up to the left here.

You cross two streams in quick succession (fill up with
water at the signposted SPRING here) just below the **Refuge
de Paliri** (**2h**). This small alpine retreat comes as a pleasant
surprise. Built of stone, with a wooden roof, it could be
an up-market shepherds' hut. It shelters on a grassy slope,
in the company of a few splendid pines — the whole
setting dwarfed by a backdrop of great granite cliffs falling
off the shoulders of the **Punta Tafunata di i Paliri**.

When you've tired of this blissfully peaceful spot,
return the same way to **Bavella** (**4h**).

# 36 TROU DE LA BOMBE

**See also photograph opposite (top)**     **Distance/time:** 6km/3.7mi; 2h

**Grade:** fairly easy, with overall ascents of under 150m/500ft; agility is required on the approach to the Trou de la Bombe.

**Equipment:** see page 50; walking boots are best; *IGN map 4253 ET*

**Access:** as Walk 35, page 123

**Short walk/picnic suggestion: Aiguilles viewpoint** (2.8km/1.7mi; 55min; easy). Follow the main walk to the 30min-point. Then retrace your steps and keep left at both forks, to return to 'Bavella par la Chapelle'.

This walk to the edge of the southern Bavella massif is shady and undemanding — a perfect outing for a warm day. But it's not lacking in drama — you can either admire the 'shell-hole' from a distance, or climb up to it!

**Start out** by following WALK 35 (page 123). About 600m from the *auberge,* fork right uphill (**10min**) on a path waymarked with red paint (30 paces before Walk 35 forks left). The path rises gently through ferns and pines. Ten minutes uphill a crossing path is signposted to the right: 'BAVELLA PAR LA CHAPELLE' (it's your return route). Turn *left* here, for 'COMPULEDDU' and 'PIANONA'. Two minutes later, at another fork, 'TROU DE LA BOMBE' is signposted down to the left. Although that is our destination, first we'll make a short detour to a pretty viewpoint.

Fork *right uphill* here for 'PIANONA', following orange waymarks. An easy ascent of eight minutes brings you to a crossing track at the top of a rise, at the setting shown opposite, a GRASSY PLATEAU (**30min**) from where you look out to the Aiguilles de Bavella — an idyllic picnic spot.

Turn left on the track and, three minutes later, fork left on a lesser track (*not* waymarked). This narrows to a path and brings you back to the main 'TROU DE LA BOMBE' path in four minutes: turn right on this wider, crossing path. The gentle undulations of this red-waymarked path bring you to a barrage of signposts at the **Bocca di Velaco** (**55min**). Cairned paths (*not* signposted) lead almost straight ahead from this pleasant clearing up to the jagged

heights of Punta Velaco and le Promontoire. But we turn *left* here. After about seven minutes, take a path climbing up to the right (red waymarking on trees). In two minutes you're just below the 'shell-hole' (**Trou de la Bombe**; **1h05min**). Red flashes show the best way to the hole itself, if you're brave.

Back at the Bocca di Velaco, follow 'BAVELLA PAR LA CHAPELLE', retracing your outgoing route. Just after crossing a stream, you are back at the sign for the Pianona detour. Go right, then, two minutes later, turn left, now following red and orange flashes to the **Chapelle de la Sainte Vierge (1h50min)** and on to **Bavella (2h)**.

*Trou de la Bombe (i Tafunu di u Compuleddu in Corse)*

## 37 CASCADE DE PISCIA DI GALLO

**Distance/time:** 2.5km/1.5mi; 1h30min

**Grade:** easy until the final descent to the bottom of the gorge (which requires scrambling on all fours). But it is not necessary to descend this path; you can see the top half of the waterfall from this point. The descent into the gorge is dangerous in wet weather. Total descent/ascent of 120m/400ft

**Equipment:** as page 50; stout shoes will suffice unless you are making the difficult descent which requires walking boots; *IGN map 4254 ET*

**Access:** 🚗 car or 🚌 (Timetable 5) to/from the snack bar 'La Cascada' on the D368 north of the Barrage d'Ospédale

**Picnic suggestion:** Follow the main walk for up to 20min; picnic either at the Ruisseau di Piscia di Gallo or up on the ridge overlooking the coast or the gorge. Adequate shade.

The Piscia di Gallo waterfall is more striking for its setting than its size, although it does fall 50m/165ft in one sheer drop, shooting straight out of a sheer face of rock. To me the setting is reminiscent of the Orient: a mountain scene painted by a Chinese master.

**Start the walk** by taking the path to the right of the walkers' signboard at the snack bar 'LA CASCADA'. Follow cairns bearing blue and white 'WATERFALL' symbols down through a forest of young pines. Just after crossing a small STREAM (**12min**), the main route veers off left. You, however, follow the path off to the right, as the waymarking indicates. A minute later you cross a wider stream at a ford (this crossing may be wet outside summer). Over the stream, watch for a path off to the right, climbing a rocky surface. (The main path continues straight on before it, too, bends right.) Taking this less-obvious path, you reach a low crest, from where you bear left. (A path forks off right here, down to another stream, the **Ruisseau di Piscia di Gallo**, the source of the waterfall. It's a quiet 'away from it all' setting, if you're already in a picnic mood.)

A bouldery landscape with heather and pines lies before you. Further along the ridge, you can see a stretch of coastline. Soon the main path comes in from the left, at a clearing used for emergency helicopter landings (**20min**; signboard; large cairn). In the rocky gulley below you on the right is the Ruisseau de Piscia di Gallo; it later widens into the Rivière de l'Oso and empties into the Gulf of Porto Vecchio. Your way heads across the rock and through the maquis. Watch the waymarking, as livestock paths also cross the path you are following.

*The Cascade de Piscia di Gallo shoots straight down a sheer rock face in a setting reminiscent of an oriental water-colour.*

Just before the descent begins you come face to face with two enormous boulders — one of them teetering on a 'thread' of rock. The path starts to descend just to the left of them. After a short distance, it bends to the right and becomes steeper. A few minutes later you pass to the right of another very large boulder and soon come to a sign, 'PASSAGE DANGEREUX' (**30min**). The top half of the **Cascade de Piscia di Gallo** is visible from here; it leaps out of a towering rock face and plummets into a gorge of dense vegetation. An impressive sight, but even more so when you're down in the gorge looking up at it.

A very rough, rocky, and steep descent follows. *Take great care. All fours are needed.* You descend under a thick canopy of vegetation, cool and dark. Dropping as far as you can *safely* go (**40min**), you still cannot reach the foot of the falls. You look through trees, to see the waterfall thunder down on to the rocks below, where three gushing arms of water cascade into a pool.

On your return, after reaching the two enormous boulders, it is possible to descend to the river and follow it upstream, before climbing up to your original route near the helicopter landing site.

Then return to the snack bar LA CASCADA (**1h30min**).

## 38 MONTE CALVA AND THE 'DIAMOND'

**Distance/time:** 7km/4.3mi; 3h (with optional detour to the Bergerie de Luviu 12km/7.5mi; 4h30min; see footnote on page 130)

**Grade:** easy-moderate, with an ascent of 386m/1270ft; stony underfoot

**Equipment:** as page 50; walking boots and sunhat recommended; *IGN map 4254 ET*

**Access:** 🚗 car or 🚌 (Timetable 5) to/from the Bocca d'Illarata (D368, 10km north of l'Ospédale)

**Short walk/picnic suggestion: Punta di u Diamanti** (easy; about 25min). See notes from the 2h35min-point on page 130. Fine picnic spots.

This walk is at its best on a clear day in spring or autumn. Monte Calva may not be an inspiring peak to climb, but from the top you will look out west as far as the Golfe de Valinco, while the eastern gulfs seem to lie at your feet. Then round off the walk in the foothills of the Punta di u Diamanti, which *is* an inspiring peak, as shown below.

**Begin** on the track opposite the sign 'BOCCA D'ILLARATA' (a sign, 'FORET TERRITORRIALE DE L'OSPEDALE', is to the right). Our goal is not yet visible. After passing to the left of a QUARRY (**10min**), keep straight ahead on the main track (cairns). Always keep to the main track, which rises gradually and becomes eroded. Churned-up earth gives away places where wild pigs have been rooting for food.

When the trees thin out (**40min**), there are wonderful views back over to the Punta di u Diamanti rising above the pass. Five minutes later you pass the rock pillars shown overleaf and then come to a large CAVE on the right (**50min**). Ignore a path off left one minute past the cave but, seven minutes later, where the track bends right, turn sharp left up a footpath marked by a large cairn. From now on you find yourself in a 'museum' of cairns, as paths thread their way left uphill, towards a gigantic red-rock

*The rocky facets of the aptly-named Punta di u Diamanti*

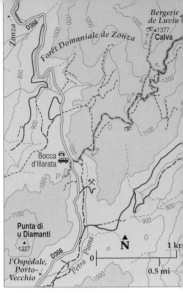

cairn on a rocky outcrop. Struggling up the stony shoulder, you pass to the right of this huge cairn and come to a TV antenna. Just to the left is the TRIG POINT on **Monte Calva** (**1h30min**), marked by two more cairns.

Return more or less the way you came. In 15 minutes you descend to a small plateau and a Y-fork. You came up the path to the left. Take the right-hand path to descend*; you're back on the track in five minutes. Turn right and descend to the **Bocca d'Illarata** (**2h35min**).

Now go down the path behind the 'BOCCA D'ILLARATA' sign on the west side of the pass. The many paths here (some cairned) allow you to ramble or scramble below the **Punta di u Diamanti**. Allow about 25 minutes (**3h**).

*This track, bulldozed over an old footpath, leads to the Bergerie de Luviu, some 2.5km to the left. if you have time (allow 1h30min return), you might like visit this isolated outpost in the pines. If so, keep *left* here.

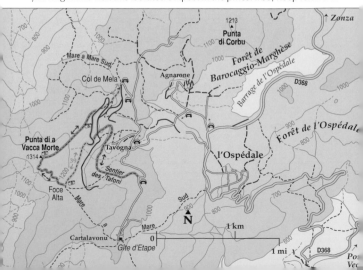

## 39 FORET DE L'OSPEDALE

**See map opposite (below)**
**Distance/time:** 4km/2.5mi; 1h 10min
**Grade:** easy ascent of 100m/325ft on gentle woodland paths
**Equipment:** no special equipment needed; *IGN map 4254 ET*
**Access:** 🚗 car to/from the Col de Mela: 1km north of l'Ospédale, turn left off the D386 for 'Agnarone, Cartalavonu, Tavogna'. See 🚗→ symbols on the map: fork left (200m), left (400m), right (1.2km), right (300m), and left (500m). Park in front of a fenced-off property (sign: 'Col de Mela 1100m'.)

**Alternative walks**
**1 Sentier des Tafoni** (time/grade as main walk). Access as main walk,

but keep *left* at the third fork (for 'Le Refuge, Cartalavonu'). Park on the right, 500m uphill, at a nature trail. Follow the posts with orange signs *and the yellow flashes,* contouring through the forest. You cross two forestry tracks and join the main walk at the 20min-point. Return the same way.
**2 Punta di a Vacca Morte** (5km/ 3mi; 2h). *For the adventurous;* walking boots recommended. Follow the main walk or Alternative walk 1 to the Foce Alta, then head up to this rocky peak. Rely on your own sense of direction or a compass (unreliable cairning).
**Picnic suggestion:** Follow the main walk for 15min (viewpoint).

---

This little-visited walk is one of the most beautiful in the south, and perfect for the whole family. Shady paths, soft with pine needles and aglow with cyclamen in spring, take you to a grassy plateau, from where the *sportifs* can forge a way up to the cross on 'Dead Cow Peak'.

**Start out** at the **Col de Mela**, where the MARE A MARE SUD footpath crosses. Facing the building, go left up a forestry track and, almost immediately, fork right on a footpath (orange flashes). Cross another track, then join it and continue to the left. By a grassy mound you enjoy a brilliant VIEW (**15min**) down over the Barrage de l'Ospédale, then pass a tall pine caught in the embrace of a massive cedar. Keep watch for your ongoing path cutting back *sharp right* (**20min**; yellow arrow). From here the Mare e Monti and the Sentier des Rochers (motif: two balancing rocks) join forces *(Alternative walk 1 joins here.)*

After crossing a stream the path emerges from the wood at a grassy plateau strewn with gnarled pines and 'wild-west' rock formations, the **Foce Alta** (**40min**). Signs point the way to a 'VUE PANORAMIQUE', to the continuing Mare e Monti via CARTALAVONU (an optional return on a steep path; see map), and to the PUNTA DI A VACCA MORTE. (Allow 35 minutes to puzzle your way to this peak; all cairning peters out! From the top, there are superb views over the gulfs of Valinco and Porto-Vecchio and Sardinia.)

Return the same way to the **Col de Mela** (**1h10min**).

# 40 BONIFACIO AND CAPO PERTUSATO

See also photographs on page 47 and cover

**Distance/time:** 9km/5.6mi; 3h10min

**Grade:** easy; a walk for all the family. Can be very windy: on such days *do not* venture near the edge of the cliff! *Almost no shade.*

**Equipment:** as page 50; stout shoes, bathing things, sun protection and plenty of water recommended; *IGN map 4255 OT*

**Access:** 🚗 or 🚌 (Timetable 19; *in high season only*) to/from Bonifacio

**Short walk/picnic suggestion: Bonifacio cliffs** (up to 2.5km/1.5mi; 45min; easy). Follow the main walk for the first 10-25min, to picnic anywhere along the magnificent limestone cliffs. *No shade.*

**B**onifacio is a must for all visitors to southern Corsica. This dramatically-sited, cliff-hanging town, with its centuries-old narrow streets is most impressive. The walk too, is quite spectacular. Wandering along the windswept cliff-tops on this southernmost tip of the island, you're virtually blinded by the chalk-white limestone bluffs and the dazzling navy blue sea that they overhang.

**Begin the walk** at the church of **St Erasme**, near the western end of the marina-side cafés in **Bonifacio**. (In the Genoese era this was the fishermen's church, since they were forbidden entry into the town.) Climb the flight of steps towards the old town. Tall, ancient buildings (with facelifts) line the steep pedestrian way. The imposing citadel walls rise high above you, on your right. Five minutes up, a magnificent view awaits you at the **Col St Roch**. You look along the sheer curving coastline of brilliant white cliffs. On clear days you can see the low hills of Sardinia rising in the southeast. The chapel here at the viewpoint marks the site of the death of the last victim of the Great Plague of 1528, which wiped out 60 per cent of the town's population.

To head out around the cliffs, climb the paved path that ascends to the left ('CIRCUIT PEDESTRE DES FALAISES'). You have a fine view back towards the strategically-sited town and over into the inlet sheltering the port. Once on the cliffs, hold onto your hats! The paving soon peters out and you're following a worn path of earth and stones. The surrounding peninsula is flat, but endless gulleys (many of them hidden from view) bite into it. Low wind-bent junipers and maquis shade the landscape in dark green hues. Far inland you can see the tail of the Montagne de Cagna.

It's very tempting to peer over the very edge of the cliffs, but *this is exceedingly dangerous*, because there's often a big overhang that could easily crumble away. There are a couple of viewpoints with protective walls;

otherwise, keep well back from the edge if it's windy, and supervise children carefully. All the way along you overlook the wind- and sea-eroded coastline — a magnificent picnic setting.

You pass the SHELL OF A BUILDING (**30min**) and fifteen minutes later join the LIGHTHOUSE ROAD (**45min**). Turn right here and, when the road forks (**55min**), head right towards the Phare (lighthouse) de Pertusato. Minutes later you circle a small gulley. Strike off right here on a path; it takes you down to the edge of the sea in eight minutes, onto smooth white tongues of limestone.

*View north to Bonifacio from the coastal path*

Take the same path back to the road and ascend past GUN BATTERIES and, a little further on, the MARITIME OBSERVATION TOWER. Crossing a crest, you get a closer look at Sardinia, only twelve kilometres away. The Iles Lavezzi form the necklace of rocky islets between the two islands. The lighthouse sits alone on the point ahead. Two or three minutes below the crest, just as the road makes a U-turn, ignore a track going almost straight ahead. But, very quickly after this, take a path off left, ascending through the hillside scrub. Squeezing through the thorny maquis, you'll see a wealth of rosemary and red-berried *Lentiscus.* Should you venture upon herds of grazing goats out here, pass them quietly. Five minutes through the scrub you rejoin the road. Turn left and, after 40m/yds, turn hard back to the right on a dirt track. Not far down the track, take the path descending the left-hand wall of a gulley that cuts down to the shore. A curious piece of coastline eaten away by wind and water awaits you. A monumental salient of limestone dominates the hilly waterfront.

When you reach the water's edge, you discover a small sandy BEACH (**1h30min**), obscured by the rocky shoreline. The small islet of St Antoine, adorned with a cross, hides behind the monumental rock. Climb the rock for another fine view of Bonifacio. A BLOWHOLE lies unnoticed to the right of the rock. Approach the edge with the utmost care, as it, too, is eaten away underneath. Pay particular attention when gale force winds batter the point here!

Return the same way to **Bonifacio (3h10min)**.* If you wish to visit the lighthouse (**Phare de Pertusato**), there's a steep path from the beach straight up to it.

*From the road junction (the 55min-point on the outward walk), you can take a path running just to the left of the road. In calm weather, you can usually follow paths all the way back to the ruin at the 30min-point.

# Index

Only geographical names are included here. For other entries, see Contents, page 3. *Italic* page numbers indicate a map, **bold** numbers a photograph (either of these may be in addition to a text reference on the same page).